Carol Bowen's

MICROWAVE COOKING FOR ONE & TWO

Carol Bowen's MICROWAVE COOKING FOR ONE & TWO

GRUB STREET · LONDON

Special thanks go to Claire James and Gail Ashton who typed and made sense of my drafted recipes and notes; to Jackie Goodwin for her testing, re-testing and double-checking at all times; to nanny Elizabeth Kempton for keeping my daughter Lucy happy, amused and out of sight as deadline date rapidly approached; and finally to my husband Peter for his amusing comments and amazing ability to be able to taste sweet before savoury and pudding before starter at a moment's notice for countless months.

Published by
Grub Street
Golden House
28–31 Great Pulteney St
London W1

First impression in hardback 1986

Photographs by James Jackson
Illustrations by Julie Carpenter

British Library Cataloguing in Publication Data

Bowen, Carol
Carol Bowen's microwave cooking for one and two.
1. Microwave cookery
I. Title
641.5'882 TX832

ISBN 0-948817-00-3

Computerset by Tradespools
Printed and bound in Italy by New Interlitho

It is some 10 years since I first dabbled with the delights of the microwave and through those years I have experienced wonderful 'highs' and depressing 'lows'. In the early heady days I truly believed that the microwave could do everything my conventional cooker could do, faster . . . and more. They proved exciting times – foods did cook fast and full of flavour but they also proved challenging times since I was determined to make it work.

Numb with microwave fatigue I took a rest and the microwave sat back for a few months, only to re-emerge as my faithful kitchen companion. For during those months I missed its speed, longed for its crisp textures, colours and flavours when cooking vegetables and wished I'd had it handy at a friend's home to show off a shortcut.

So slowly over the years, by trial and error I hope I have the microwave in perspective – as a loyal adjunct to my conventional cooker, refrigerator and freezer. I use it to its best effect with all three. My casseroles which could be cooked in the microwave but somehow lacked that 'long-simmered' flavour now start in the microwave and finish in the conventional oven (I still save up to 1 hour on time but don't sacrifice any flavour); vegetables never see a saucepan or hob, they are always cooked in the microwave to just-tender perfection; sauces too are cooked in a jug to emerge velvety smooth; and meats brown and cook tender in my indispensable browning dish.

Speed and flavour were often the judging factors and the microwave proved good in both areas – but never better than when the dish was intended for less than 4 servings and when convenience coupled with flavour played a leading role. So again, without deliberate thought, the microwave marvelled in precise areas by its own virtues – usually in cooking for 1 and 2 servings when speed is important but flavour is paramount.

My collection of both time-honoured and newly-developed favourites is here for you to enjoy – they represent years of mid-week and special occasion eating for my husband and myself; numerous occasions when a speedy dish was required to feed a girlfriend at lunch; many occasions when I was eating alone and countless times when I cooked for the pure pleasure of it. I hope you will enjoy my selection.

AT A GLANCE MENU PLANNER

INTRODUCTION

STARTERS AND SNACKS

SNACKS

MAIN MEALS

FISH

MEAT

POULTRY

VEGETARIAN

VEGETABLES, SALADS AND SIDE DISHES

SALADS

SIDE DISHES

SAUCES, BUTTERS, STUFFINGS AND DRESSINGS

BUTTERS

STUFFINGS

DRESSINGS

DESSERTS

Introduction

WHAT ARE MICROWAVES?

The chances are, if you are a freezer-owner or busy cook, you will have welcomed the arrival of the microwave oven. For with a microwave to help, you will be able to speedily cook, defrost and reheat food in seconds instead of the usual minutes or hours of conventional cooking. But what are microwaves and where do they come from?

The mechanics of the microwave oven are no more magical than a television or radio. Inside the microwave is a magnetron vacuum tube – this is the 'heart' of the microwave and converts ordinary household electrical energy into high frequency electro-magnetic waves, called microwaves. Once produced, the microwaves are then directed into the oven cavity, through a wave guide and stirred, by a fan, for even distribution.

These waves are then either reflected, pass through or are absorbed by different materials. Metals reflect them (so cooking utensils must be non-metallic), glass, pottery, paper and most plastics allow them to pass through (which is why they make ideal cooking utensils) and foods absorb them. The microwaves are absorbed by the moisture in food, causing the food molecules to vibrate rapidly, thus producing heat to cook food. The speed at which microwaves cause the molecules to vibrate is millions of times per second – producing an intense heat that cooks extra fast.

It is a completely different method of cooking food compared with conventional methods – especially since dishes remain cool, metals cannot be used and timings are extra speedy . . . and as a result different cooking procedures and techniques are called into action.

THE MICROWAVE COOKER

All basic models are pretty much the same in design. They consist of a cabinet, magnetron, wave guide, wave stirrer, power supply, power cord and controls. Some have special extra features like automatic defrost, variable power control, turntable, integral thermometer or temperature probe and browning or crisping elements. Varying only slightly in design, they all work in the same way – microwaves are produced in the magnetron and are passed into the oven cavity through the wave guide to be stirred by a fan. Once there, the microwaves are safely contained in the cavity since the base and walls are made of metal and deflect the microwaves into the food. All cooker doors and frames are fitted with special seals as an extra safety measure to ensure microwaves stay in the cooker. In addition, all microwave cookers have one or more cut-out devices so that the flow of microwaves stops automatically whenever the door is opened or indeed if the door has not been shut properly.

Within the vast selection of microwave ovens available three basic models can be identified:

Portable microwave ovens

At the present time these are the most popular ovens on the market. Almost as light and portable as a TV they simply require a 13- or 15-amp plug for use and will happily sit on a convenient work surface, trolley or other firm, stable surface for operation.

Double oven cooker

A few microwave models are available teamed up, and in the same unit as a conventional cooker – here the microwave acts as a second or double oven. Most are built-in but a few are available free-standing.

Combination cookers

Deemed to be the fastest growing sector of the microwave oven market and certainly worthy of interest, these ovens have the facility to cook by both microwave and conventionally in one operation and in one unit – also in tandem or sequence with each other. Some models offer further choices with fan-assistance, grilling and automatic roasting controls linked with the microwave.

All that is required to install a portable microwave oven is a fused power socket. Manufacturers also recommend that you place the microwave on a stable surface and have adequate ventilation. It is therefore possible to site the microwave in a multitude of places. I place mine on a stable trolley so that I can wheel it from room to room as required – giving useful flexibility of cooking.

If you plan to build-in your microwave to kitchen units then ensure you buy the correct fixing kit or housing unit. Make sure there is adequate venting, and always check your microwave handbook for any special instructions.

OVEN CLEANING

Since the walls to the oven cavity of the microwave remain cool during cooking, cleaning is often a quick-wipe operation. Food does not have the opportunity to bake-on. Simply wipe, at regular intervals or as spills occur, with a damp soapy cloth – after disconnecting the oven from the electrical supply. Remove and wash oven trays, shelving and bases if possible in the same way, or according to the manufacturer's instructions.

Wipe over the outside surfaces and the door of the oven regularly but do not allow water to seep into the vents. If possible, also clean any air filters or stirrer fan guard according to the instructions in your handbook.

Stale cooking smells can be removed by boiling a solution of 3 parts water to 1 part lemon juice in a bowl in the microwave for about 5 minutes, then wipe with a cloth to dry.

Also remember to have the microwave checked or serviced by a qualified engineer every 12 months, or as recommended by the manufacturer.

Do not operate the cooker when it is empty. For safety, place a cup of water in the cooker when it is not in use. If the cooker is accidentally switched on the water will absorb the energy – there is then negligible risk of damaging the magnetron.

FACTORS WHICH AFFECT MICROWAVE COOKING

Starting temperature of food

Foods which are cooked from room temperature will take less time than foods which are frozen or chilled. Cooking times given in these recipes refer to a starting temperature of foods as they are normally stored, unless otherwise stated.

Density of food

The denser the food, the longer it takes to cook. Heavy, dense foods like meat or potatoes will take longer to cook than light, porous foods like sponge cakes and puddings. For the same reason a solid, dense mass of meat like a joint will take longer to cook than the same meat minced or chopped prior to cooking.

Composition of food

Foods which are high in fats and sugars will cook faster than foods high in liquid because fats and sugars absorb microwave energy more readily. They also reach higher temperatures during

GUIDE TO COMPARATIVE MICROWAVE OVEN CONTROL SETTINGS

Settings used in these recipes	Settings variations on popular microwave ovens			Approximate % power input	Approximate power output in watts	Cooking times (in minutes) (for times greater than 10 minutes simply add together the figures in the appropriate columns)									
	1 keep warm	low	2	25%	150W	4	8	12	16	20	24	28	32	36	40
LOW	2 simmer		3	30%	200W	3¼	6¾	10	13¼	16¾	20	23¼	26¾	30	33¼
DEFROST	3 stew	medium/low	4	40%	250W	2½	5	7½	10	12½	15	17½	20	22½	25
	4 defrost	medium	5	50%	300W	2	4	6	8	10	12	14	16	18	20
MEDIUM	5 bake	medium	6	60%	400W	1¾	3¼	5	6¾	8¼	10	12	13¼	15	16½
	6 roast	high	7–8	75%	500–500W	1¼	2¾	4	5¼	6¾	8	9¼	10¾	12	13¼
HIGH	7 full/high	normal	10	100%	700W	1	2	3	4	5	6	7	8	9	10

cooking than water-based foods. It therefore takes more time to cook foods which are high in moisture like meats and vegetables, than it does to cook those with little moisture like cakes and breads.

Quantity of food

As the volume or quantity of food being cooked in the microwave increases, the cooking time increases. If you double the amount of food, the time will increase by about one-half as much again.

Size and shape of food

Smaller pieces of food will cook more quickly than larger pieces, and uniformly shaped pieces cook more evenly than irregularly shaped ones. With unevenly shaped pieces, the thinner parts will cook faster than the thicker areas and should be placed towards the centre of the dish where they receive less energy. Ideally, portions of food that are of the same size and shape cook most evenly. It is also important to remember that round and ring shapes cook more evenly than square, oval or rectangular shapes. With the latter the energy seems to concentrate in the corners and can cause charring – to overcome this effect, protect the corners with small pieces of foil to shield them from the energy.

Height in the oven

Areas that are closest to any source of energy cook faster than those further away and this also occurs in the microwave. Depending on its design your microwave may cook faster near the floor or roof. Rotating, turning over and stirring of foods will minimise this effect.

Bones in meat

Bone in meat conducts heat – therefore meat next to the bone in a joint will cook first. Wherever possible, it is wise to bone and roll meat for even cooking. If you don't, then remember to shield the meat next to the bone halfway through the cooking time to prevent over-cooking.

TECHNIQUES

As with any new appliance, and certainly with one that has an unfamiliar cooking action, there are a few simple techniques to follow to ensure success:

Stirring

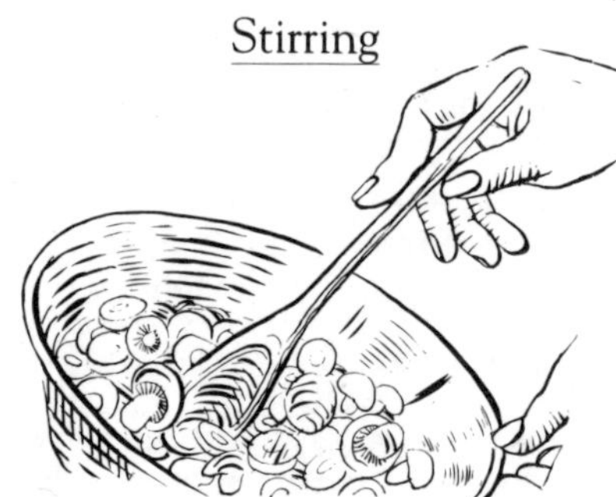

Stirring is an operation that is carried out when cooking conventionally and is also applied when cooking by microwave. Conventionally we stir from the bottom of the pan to the top but with a microwave this is from the outside to the centre of a dish for even cooking. Precise stirring instructions will be given in a recipe if it is important, if not a simple stir halfway through the cooking time will suffice.

Rotating

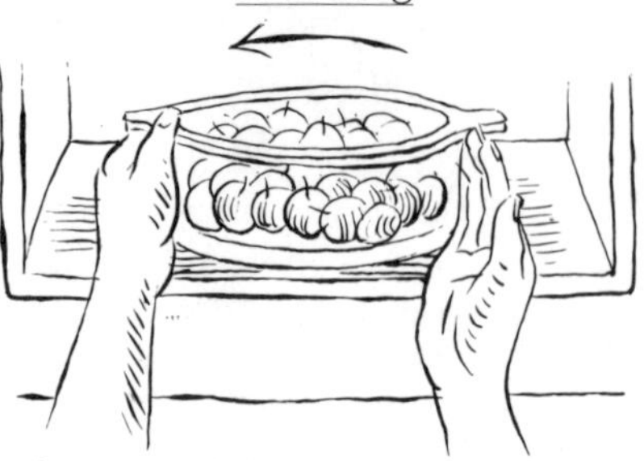

If your model of microwave has a turntable then this cooking technique becomes redundant. If it hasn't then a simple quarter or half-turn of a dish at regular intervals during the cooking time will ensure even cooking when a dish cannot be stirred or turned over.

Turning over

Many large dense items of food like potatoes often appreciate turning over after about half of the microwave cooking time to ensure good results.

Arranging

The careful arranging of food in a dish for microwave cooking can mean the difference between a perfectly cooked ingredient and an adequately cooked one. For success follow the guidelines below:

- try to cook foods of an even or similar size together and if possible arrange in a ring pattern leaving the centre empty.

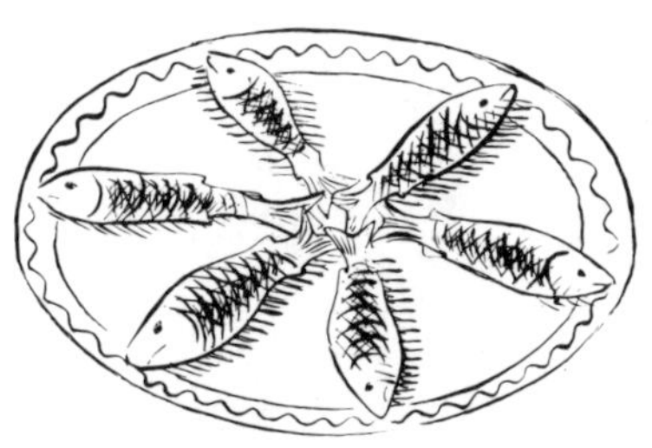

- if foods are of an irregular shape, like chops, spears of broccoli or small fish then arrange the thicker sections to the outside of the dish where they will receive the most energy to cook.
- for plated meals ensure the food is spread evenly across the plate or that thicker pieces of meat or vegetables are to the outer edge where they receive most energy.
- wherever possible ensure the depth of the food in a dish is even – if not, stir or rearrange to compensate for this.

Rearranging

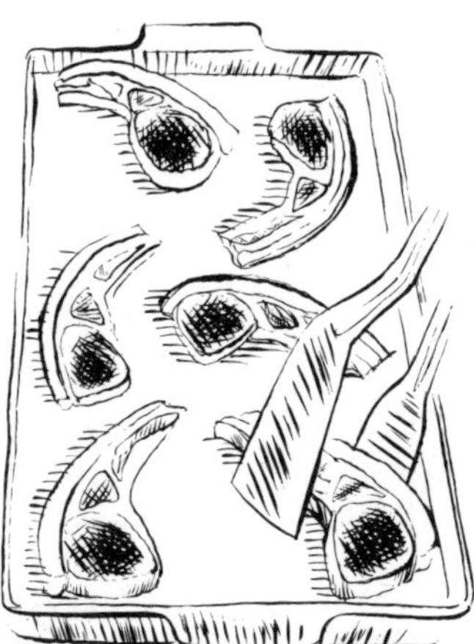

Rearranging foods cooked in the microwave will also ensure evenly-cooked results – even if your microwave has a turntable. Once during the cooking time is usually sufficient – moving foods from the outside of the dish to the centre and vice versa.

Shielding

As with conventional cooking some parts of foods are more vulnerable to over-cooking than others. Wing tips of poultry, fish heads and tails, duck tail-ends and the narrow ends of legs of pork or lamb are examples. In such cases it is considered acceptable to introduce small strips of aluminium foil to protect such areas (although do check in your microwave handbook).

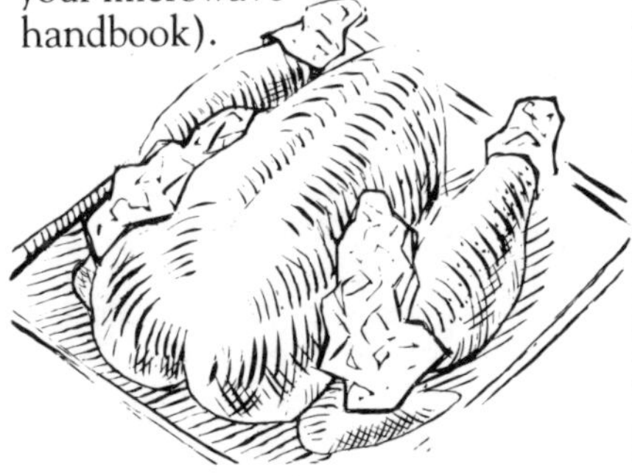

This is the only time when metal may be introduced into a typical microwave oven and it is important to make sure it does not touch the oven walls. Position on the food for half of the cooking time and secure with wooden cocktail sticks if necessary.

Covering and wrapping

Drying out, spattering of walls and slower cooking times than needed can all be eliminated by covering or wrapping foods for the microwave. Covering will 'lock-in' and contain juices and speed up cooking times by trapping heat-retaining steam.

There are several ways to cover or wrap foods for cooking:

- use a tight-fitting purpose-made lid or an improvised saucer or plate for the same effect.
- use double-strength plastic cook bags especially for meat and vegetables but replace the metal ties with rubber bands, string or plastic clips.

- cover with a tight membrane of cling film but puncture or turn back a vent to prevent a 'ballooning' effect. Take care however when removing since it will trap steam which burns.

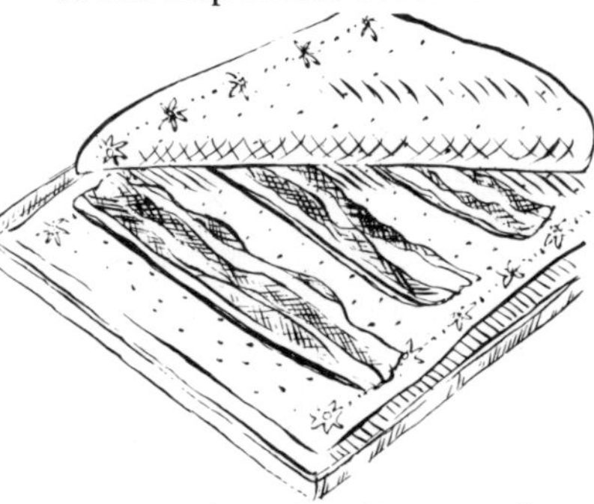

- use absorbent kitchen towel as a base to stand food on or as a cover for the same. It is especially good for absorbing excess moisture in foods that appreciate crisping like potatoes, bacon and bread. It is also invaluable for drying herbs and when dampened for reheating and steaming pancakes and shellfish.

Observing standing times

Food still continues to cook by conduction when microwave energy has been turned off. This is not a special action devoted to the microwave alone – the same action happens to a lesser degree with conventional cooking and it must be catered for. For this reason it is important to err on the side of safety and undercook rather than overcook food to allow for this action.

Removing excess cooking juices

Any juices that seep from a food will continue to attract microwave energy – if these juices are considerable then it is advisable to remove them with a bulb baster regularly during cooking so that they do not prolong cooking times appreciably.

Releasing pressure in foods
Foods with tight skins or membranes like sausages, kidneys, giblets, jacket potatoes, baked apples and egg yolks must be lightly pricked prior to cooking or they are liable to burst or explode. For the same reason boil-in-the-bag pouches and cling film must be cut or vented – this is because of the tremendous amount of pressure that develops within such quickly cooked food.

Browning foods
As a result of little applied surface heat over short cooking times – foods cooked in the microwave do not readily brown. To encourage and assist or disguise the browning process try one of the following tips if liked:

- grill foods like gratins and roasts before or after microwave cooking.
- use a special microwave browning dish especially for foods like chops, steaks, fried eggs, toasted sandwiches, stir-frys and chicken portions.
- buy or make your own browning mix to coat foods – paprika, toasted breadcrumbs, crushed crisps, soy sauce, Worcestershire sauce and soup mixes are good ideas that work well.

- bacon due to its high fat content, browns readily so can be laid over poultry or roasts.
- baked items like cakes, biscuits and breads could be coated with toasted coconut, chocolate vermicelli, chopped nuts, chopped glacé fruits, poppy seeds, herbs and many dark coloured spices.
- ice or frost a cake or baked item after cooking.
- glaze ham, poultry or game with a fruit preserve or marmalade to add colour.

A FEW RESTRICTIONS

The following foods do not cook well in the microwave:

Eggs in shells
These are liable to explode due to the build-up of pressure within the shell.

Popcorn
This is too dry to attract microwave energy.

Batter recipes
Items like Yorkshire puddings, soufflés, pancakes and crêpes need conventional cooking to become crisp and firm.

Conventional meringues
These should be cooked in the conventional oven.

Deep fat frying
This is not recommended since it requires prolonged heating, it is difficult to control the temperature of the fat and food may burn.

Liquids in bottles
Check that bottles do not have too narrow necks or built-up pressure may cause them to shatter.

DISHES AND UTENSILS

Without doubt, the range of cooking utensils that can be used in the microwave oven is wider than those used for cooking conventionally.

A few exceptions do, however, exist. Most manufacturers object to the use of metal. Even small amounts in the oven will reflect the microwaves so that they do not penetrate the food to be cooked. Therefore, avoid metal dishes, baking trays and metal baking tins, foil dishes, cast-iron casseroles, plates and china trimmed with a metallic design, any dish with a metal screw or attachment and the paper-coated metal ties often found with freezer and cook bags.

Glass, pottery and china
Oven-proof and plain glass, pottery and china are all suitable. Be sure to check that they do not have any metallic trim, screws or handles, and if using a pottery dish that it is non-porous.

Paper
For low heat and short cooking times, such as thawing, reheating or very short prime cooking, and for foods with a low fat, sugar or water content, paper is a good

utensil. Napkins, paper towels, cups, cartons, paper freeze wrap and the paper pulp board often used for meat packaging are all suitable. (Paper towels are especially useful for cooking fatty foods, since they absorb excess fats and oils and can be used to prevent splattering on the walls of the oven.)

Wax-coated paper cups and plates should be avoided since the high temperature of the food will cause the wax to melt; they can, however, be used for defrosting cold items like frozen cakes and desserts.

Plastics

'Dishwasher Safe' is a useful indication as to whether or not a plastic is suitable for the microwave. Plastic dishes and containers, unless made of a thermoplastic material, should not be used for cooking food with a high fat or sugar content, since the heat of the food may cause the plastic to melt or lose its shape. Plastic film and devices like boil-in-bags work well. Pierce the film or bag before cooking to allow steam to escape, and take care when removing the plastic film in case any steam remains. Do not attempt to cook in thin plastic bags as they will not withstand the heat of the food. Thicker storage bags are acceptable. Use elastic bands, string or non-metal ties to secure the bags loosely before cooking. Melamine is not recommended for microwave cooking since it absorbs enough microwave energy to cause charring.

Cotton and linen

Napkins are ideal for short warming or reheating procedures like reheating bread rolls for serving. It is important only to use cotton or linen containing no synthetic fibres.

Wooden bowls and basketware

These are only suitable for short reheating purposes, otherwise the wood or wicker will tend to char, dry out or crack.

Roasting bags

A very clean, convenient way of cooking many foods. This is particularly true of meats, since browning takes place more readily within them than in other plastic bags. However, the metal ties must be replaced with elastic bands or string. Snip a couple of holes in the bag to aid the escape of steam.

Microwave containers

With the increased popularity of microwave cooking comes a host of special innovations in microwave cookware. Several ranges manufactured from polythene, polystyrene and thermoplastics are now widely available and come in a comprehensive range of shapes and sizes.

Thermometers

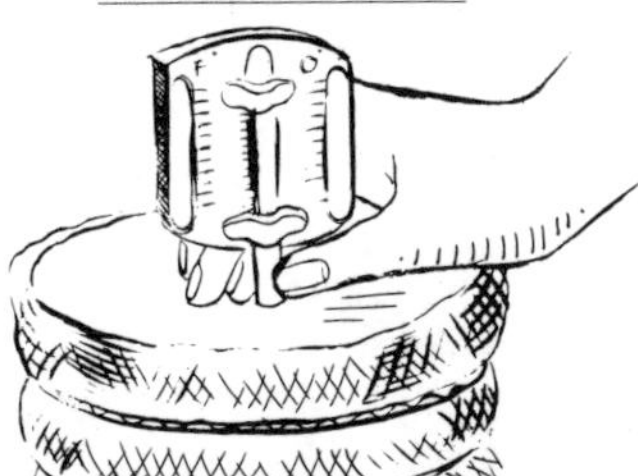

Ones made specially for microwave ovens are available but can be used in an oven only when specified by that oven's manufacturer. To take the temperature reading with a standard meat thermometer, remove the food from the oven, insert the thermometer into the thickest portion of food and let it stand for about 10 minutes to register the internal temperature. If more cooking is needed, remove the thermometer and return the meat to the oven. Some newer ovens have an automatic cooking control, a temperature sensing probe, that can be inserted into a roast or other food while in the oven. When the food reaches a precise temperature, the oven turns itself off automatically.

Browning dishes

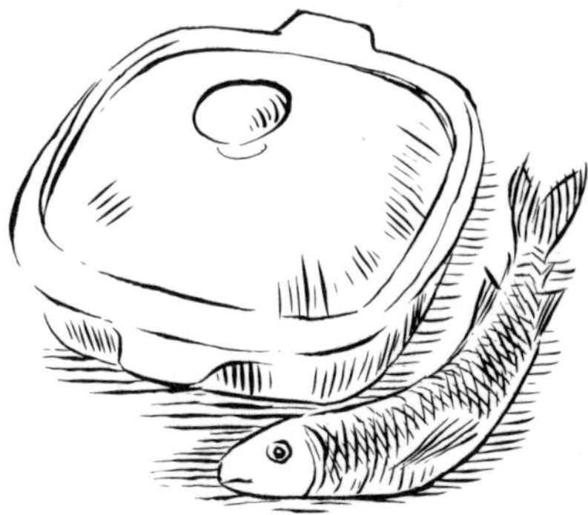

Available from most microwave dealers, these duplicate the conventional browning and searing processes of conventional cooking. Especially useful for pre-browning meat, poultry and fish, they can also be used for 'frying' eggs and sandwiches, and browning vegetables. The browning dish, made of a glass-ceramic substance with a special coating that absorbs microwave energy, is preheated in the microwave until the base coating changes colour, usually about 8 minutes on HIGH or full power. The food is then placed on the dish to brown and turned to sear

the remaining sides. Preheating times and browning or searing times differ according to the food being cooked and the power output of the oven. Always follow the manufacturer's instructions.

Remember

If you are going to cook food in both the microwave and the conventional oven, be sure to use an oven-proof dish. Here's a simple test:

Fill a heatproof glass cup with water and place in the utensil being checked. Place the utensil in the microwave oven and cook for 1¼ minutes. If the water is warm in the cup and the utensil is cool, go ahead and use the utensil. If the utensil is warm or even hot and the water is still cool, or barely lukewarm, do not use it for microwave cooking.

The shape of dish to use

After checking the material of the dish or utensil, consider its shape, too. Ideally, the more regular the shape the better it is suited to microwave cooking, e.g. a round shape is better than an oval. A straight-sided container is better than a curved one, as the microwaves can penetrate more evenly. A large shallow dish is better than a small deep one as the food offers a greater surface area to the microwaves.

DEFROSTING

During the early introductory years of the domestic microwave it was frequently referred to as 'the unfreezer' since one of the major advantages and bonuses of owning a microwave was its ability to defrost food quickly and efficiently.

Capitalising on this effect many microwave manufacturers have introduced a special DEFROST control or button to ensure good defrosting microwave action. This control programmes the microwave to introduce just the right amount of energy to defrost food without cooking it – it does so by turning on and off the power at regular intervals.

It is possible to simulate this action by turning a microwave without such a control manually on and off at regular intervals with rest periods in between but is rarely as successful and can be time-consuming.

Defrosting tips

- Defrost food slowly – never try to hurry the process or there is a danger of cooking the food or drying it out unnecessarily.
- Frozen foods wrapped in freezer foil or foil containers should be stripped of their covering and placed in a suitable dish for the microwave.

- Separate sausage links, blocks of foods and stacked items like layered pancakes and burgers as they defrost.
- As with cooking, prick, slash or vent membranes like cling film before defrosting.
- Turn foods over, stir or rearrange to ensure even defrosting at least once.
- Remove excess drip or thaw juices with a bulb baster during defrosting.
- Remove giblets from poultry and game cavities when they have thawed.
- Remove metal lids and open cartons before defrosting.

- Crisp items like breads, cakes and biscuits will appreciate sitting on absorbent kitchen towel during defrosting.
- Break up blocks of meat and fish and rearrange during defrosting or remove when thawed.
- Take into account the residual heat action of the microwave by defrosting large roasts and poultry birds until just icy – after standing for some 10–15 minutes they will defrost to a chilled state.

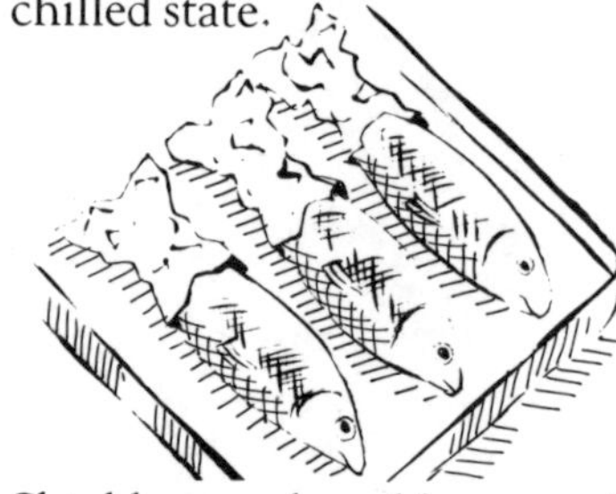

- Shield any vulnerable areas of foods like fish tails, poultry wings and chop bones with foil during defrosting as in cooking.
- Shield any parts of foods that are defrosting unnecessarily

faster than others with small strips of foil – position on the food with wooden cocktail sticks.

- If you intend to defrost and cook in one operation straight from the freezer then follow all the guidelines on stirring, turning, rotating and rearranging foods, not forgetting to allow a standing time too.

REHEATING

Most foods will reheat in the microwave cooker without loss of quality, flavour, colour and some nutrients. For best results follow the guidelines below:

- Arrange foods on a plate for reheating so that the thicker, denser and meatier portions are to the outer edge.

- Cover foods when reheating with a layer of cling film if there is no lid to retain moisture.
- When reheating, observe the standing time action to make maximum use of the microwave energy and to prevent overcooking.

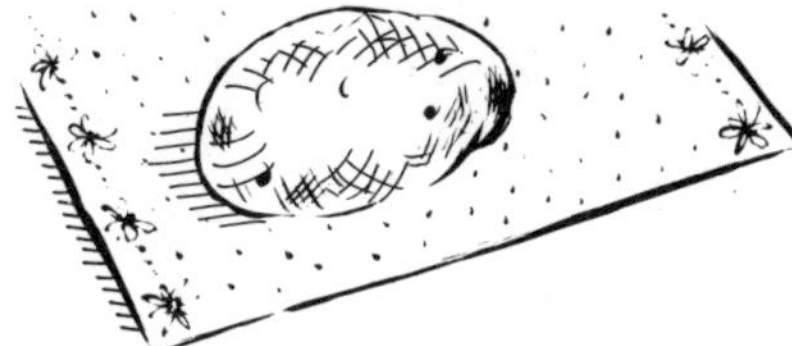

- When reheating potatoes in their jackets, breads, pastry items and other moist foods, place them on a sheet of paper towel so that it may absorb the moisture.

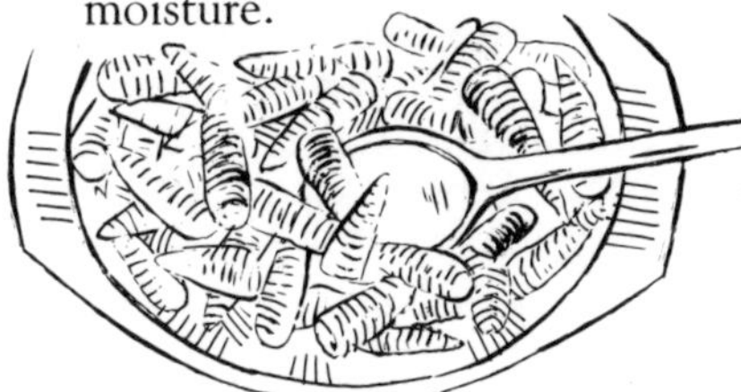

- Stir foods regularly while reheating. If stirring is not possible, then rotate the food or dish or re-arrange it.

MEAL AND MENU PLANNING

As a general rule for microwave cooking, cook the main course first. Most meat, poultry and fish dishes, especially those cooked in sauces, do improve upon standing and roasts are often easier to carve. If wrapped in aluminium foil during their standing time, they will often require no further reheating.

Obviously, cook foods that require a long standing time first. Last-minute or quick-cooking dishes can be cooked during that standing time.

For ease of preparation and cooking, prepare starters and desserts well ahead and reheat if necessary just before serving. A pudding that needs little attention can often be cooked while you are eating the starter and main course.

Menu planning and serving food perfectly cooked is an art that comes with experience. Your microwave cooker will help you through this trial and error time if you err on the side of safety. Dishes that have become lukewarm will quickly reheat with perfect freshness rather than having a dried-out look. Certainly until you have got the measure of your microwave do not attempt to reheat, thaw or even cook more than one dish in the oven at the same time – it is easy to overestimate the time required and forget the composition of the dish so that foods cook unevenly.

ADAPTING RECIPES AND SCALING DOWN TO SERVE 1 & 2

Many of your favourite family recipes can be converted for use in the microwave simply by adjusting, and often shortening, the recipe cooking time. The ideal way to start to convert a recipe is to study the recipe carefully and check whether there are any familiar techniques in its method such as roasting, steaming or poaching that you can easily convert. Check that all the ingredients included can be cooked in the microwave and refer to procedures and times from other standard microwave

recipes to work out your cooking times.

The following checklist will help you with conversion, but use it only as a guideline – rely upon your own judgement for best results.

- In general terms, foods cooked in the microwave take about one-quarter to one-third of the time they take when cooking conventionally. But do, however, allow for standing times.
- Check the cooking process regularly. Stir and rearrange foods if they appear to be cooking unevenly.
- Use less liquids when cooking items like stews, casseroles and soups and in cooking vegetables.
- Foods tend to rise higher during microwave cooking so, in general, choose larger containers.
- Reduce flavourings like herbs and spices by about one-third since the flavours of these seem to be brought out more strongly by microwave cooking.
- Wherever possible, cut food into small, even-sized pieces so that they are small and uniform for quick cooking.

Many microwave recipes produced by manufacturers are geared to serving 4 or more – but don't despair and discard your handbook, for such recipes can be halved, quartered or reduced further.

As a general guideline:

- If you wish to make a recipe for 4 serve only 2 then halve the amount of each ingredient given and microwave for about two-thirds of the given cooking time.
- If you wish to make a recipe for 4 serve only 1 then quarter the amount of each ingredient given and microwave for about one-third of the given cooking time.
- Always err on the side of safety by undercooking rather than overcooking, especially with delicate egg, fish or cream dishes.
- Choose smaller cooking dishes but stir, turn, rotate or re-arrange just as frequently.
- Leave to stand for 3–5 minutes after cooking to observe standing times rather than the 5–10 minutes usually recommended.

GUIDE TO THE RECIPES

All recipes have been tried, tested and developed for serving 1 or 2 people – however, some of the sauce recipes would prove too small and unworkable if reduced further. Any of these can be stored in the refrigerator for up to 24 hours then reheated for serving with other dishes.

All recipes in this book were created and tested using microwave ovens with a maximum power output of 700 watts. The ovens also had variable power and the descriptions used refer to the following power outputs:
HIGH = 700 watts or 100%
MEDIUM = 400 watts or 60%
DEFROST = 250 watts or 40%
LOW = 200 watts or 30%

The chart on page 9 gives the approximate power input in watts at these levels and their relative cooking times.

The microwave ovens used for testing also had a turntable facility – if yours does not then follow the rules on turning, rotating and re-arranging in the introductory chapter.

Metric measurements may vary from one recipe to another within the book and it is essential to follow *either* metric or Imperial. The recipes have been carefully balanced to get the very best results using only one set of measures and cannot be interchanged.

Note that unless otherwise stated flour is of the plain variety, eggs used refer to size 3 and all spoon quantities are measured level.

Some of the recipes are coded as a guide to whether the recipes freezes well, can be made with storecupboard ingredients or made with food leftovers. Check the codes below for accuracy:

Freezability

Indicates that a dish freezes well and indeed is worth making in bulk for freezer storage. Indication of freezer life is also given and defrosting and reheating times if appropriate.

Storecupboard standby

Indicates that a recipe can be easily made on the spur of the moment from a well-stocked storecupboard, refrigerator or freezer.

Save and savour

Indicates that the main ingredient in a recipe may be a leftover ingredient – cooked chicken, ham or rice for example.

Starters & Snacks

COUNTRY PÂTÉ

A simple chicken liver pâté made all the more special by using ready-blended herbs and garlic butter.

ONE		TWO
50 g/2 oz	**chicken livers, trimmed**	100 g/4 oz
½	**small onion, peeled and chopped**	1
25 g/1 oz	**savoury herbs and garlic butter**	50 g/2 oz

ONE

1. Place the chicken livers, onion and half of the butter in a bowl. Cover and microwave on HIGH for 1–1½ minutes until cooked. Mash with a fork until as smooth as possible. Spoon into a small ramekin or dish.

2. Place the remaining butter in a dish and microwave on HIGH for ¼ minute to melt. Spoon over the pâté and chill until set.

3. Serve cold with warm toast fingers and a salad garnish.

TWO

1. Place the chicken livers, onion and half of the butter in a bowl. Cover and microwave on HIGH for 1½–2 minutes until cooked. Mash with a fork until as smooth as possible. Spoon into a small ramekin or dish.

2. Place the remaining butter in a dish and microwave on HIGH for ¼ minute to melt. Spoon over the pâté and chill until set.

3. Serve cold with warm toast fingers and a salad garnish.

LEANLINE CHICKEN AND ORANGE PÂTÉ

Calorie counters and pound watchers will be pleased to note that this tasty pâté costs only 140 calories from a daily allowance. Serve with raw vegetable sticks or toasted low-calorie bread.

ONE		TWO
7 g/¼ oz	**low-fat spread**	15 g/½ oz
½	**small onion, peeled and chopped**	1
50 g/2 oz	**cooked chicken, skin removed and chopped**	100 g/4 oz
7.5 ml/1½ tsp	**unsweetened orange juice**	15 ml/1 tbsp
5 ml/1 tsp	**finely chopped fresh parsley**	10 ml/2 tsp
45 ml/3 tbsp	**natural yogurt**	75 ml/5 tbsp
25 g/1 oz	**button mushrooms, wiped and sliced**	50 g/2 oz
¼	**small green pepper, cored, seeded and finely chopped**	½
	salt and freshly ground black pepper	

ONE

1. Place the low-fat spread and onion in a bowl. Cover and microwave on HIGH for ¾–1 minute.
2. Place the onion mixture, chicken and orange juice in a blender and process on a low speed until finely chopped.
3. Add the parsley and yogurt and blend again to mix.
4. Remove from the blender and fold in the mushrooms, green pepper and salt and pepper to taste.
5. Spoon into a small dish and chill thoroughly before serving with raw vegetable sticks or toast.

TWO

1. Place the low-fat spread and onion in a bowl. Cover and microwave on HIGH for 1–1½ minutes.
2. Place the onion mixture, chicken and orange juice in a blender and process on a low speed until finely chopped.
3. Add the parsley and yogurt and blend again to mix.
4. Remove from the blender and fold in the mushrooms, green pepper and salt and pepper to taste.
5. Spoon into a small dish and chill thoroughly before serving with raw vegetable sticks or toast.

SAVE AND SAVOUR

Leanline Chicken and Orange Pâté is a tasty way to use up cooked leftover chicken or turkey.

See photograph on page 26·27

QUICK KIPPER PÂTÉ

A lemony kipper pâté that is best served chilled with warm Melba toast.

ONE		TWO
50 g/2 oz	**boneless kipper fillets**	100 g/4 oz
15 g/½ oz	**softened butter**	25 g/1 oz
2.5 ml/½ tsp	**finely grated lemon rind**	5 ml/1 tsp
	pinch of ground nutmeg	
	salt and freshly ground black pepper	

ONE

1. Place the kipper fillets in a small bowl and microwave on HIGH for 1–1½ minutes or until cooked.
2. Remove any skin and discard. Add the butter, lemon rind, nutmeg and salt and pepper to taste. Mash well with a fork until well blended.
3. Spoon into a small ramekin or dish and chill until set.
4. Serve lightly chilled with Melba toast.

TWO

1. Place the kipper fillets in a small bowl and microwave on HIGH for 2–2½ minutes or until cooked.
2. Remove any skin and discard. Add the butter, lemon rind, nutmeg and salt and pepper to taste. Mash well with a fork until well blended.
3. Spoon into a small ramekin or dish and chill until set.
4. Serve lightly chilled with Melba toast.

PRAWNS IN SPICY GARLIC BUTTER

Large unshelled Mediterranean prawns are best for this starter, but if unavailable use peeled prawns instead.

ONE		TWO
7.5 ml/1½ tsp	**olive oil**	15 ml/1 tbsp
7 g/¼ oz	**butter**	15 g/½ oz
1	**garlic cloves, peeled and thinly sliced**	2
1.25 ml/¼ tsp	**ground paprika**	2.5 ml/½ tsp
1.25 ml/¼ tsp	**ground cumin**	2.5 ml/½ tsp
	pinch of ground ginger	
100 g/4 oz	**large unshelled Mediterranean prawns**	225 g/8 oz
7.5 ml/1½ tsp	**chopped fresh parsley**	15 ml/1 tbsp
7.5 ml/1½ tsp	**snipped chives**	15 ml/1 tbsp

ONE

1. Place the oil, butter and garlic in a shallow cooking dish and microwave on HIGH for ½–¾ minute until the butter is melted.
2. Stir in the paprika, cumin and ginger, blending well.
3. Add the prawns and toss well to coat in the spicy garlic butter.
4. Microwave on HIGH for 2 minutes, stirring twice.
5. Stir in the parsley and chives and serve at once, with French bread.

TWO

1. Place the oil, butter and garlic in a shallow cooking dish and microwave on HIGH for 1–1¼ minutes until the butter is melted.
2. Stir in the paprika, cumin and ginger, blending well.
3. Add the prawns and toss well to coat in the spicy garlic butter.
4. Microwave on HIGH for 3–4 minutes, stirring twice.
5. Stir in the parsley and chives and serve at once, with French bread.

POTTED SHRIMPS

This is a recipe for potted shrimps with a difference – shrimps are mixed with cooked whiting or plaice then butter and spices. It is best eaten with toast or thinly sliced brown bread.

ONE		TWO
50 g/2 oz	**whiting or plaice fillet**	100 g/4 oz
10 ml/2 tsp	**water**	15 ml/1 tbsp
40 g/1½ oz	**butter**	75 g/3 oz
	pinch of cayenne pepper	
	dash of anchovy essence	
50 g/2 oz	**peeled shrimps**	100 g/4 oz
	lemon slices and parsley sprigs, to garnish	

ONE

1. Place the fish and water in a bowl. Cover and microwave on HIGH for 1 minute until cooked.
2. Drain and flake the fish then mash or pound until smooth with the butter, cayenne pepper and anchovy essence.
3. Microwave on HIGH for 1–1½ minutes until melted and hot. Stir in the shrimps, blending well.
4. Spoon into a small serving dish and chill until set.
5. Garnish with lemon slices and parsley sprigs and serve lightly chilled with toast or brown bread.

TWO

1. Place the fish and water in a bowl. Cover and microwave on HIGH for 1½–2 minutes until cooked.
2. Drain and flake the fish then mash or pound until smooth with the butter, cayenne pepper and anchovy essence.
3. Microwave on HIGH for 2–3 minutes until melted and hot. Stir in the shrimps, blending well.
4. Spoon into two small serving dishes and chill until set.
5. Garnish with lemon slices and parsley sprigs and serve lightly chilled with toast or brown bread.

MUSHROOMS À LA GRECQUE

A light mushroom starter with wine and tomatoes. Serve cold with warm crusty bread.

ONE		TWO
½	small onion, peeled and finely chopped	1
½	medium carrot, peeled and finely chopped	1
5 ml/1 tsp	olive oil	10 ml/2 tsp
30 ml/2 tbsp	dry white wine	60 ml/4 tbsp
1	bouquet garni	1
50 g/2 oz	button mushrooms, wiped	100 g/4 oz
2	tomatoes, skinned, seeded and chopped	4
	salt and freshly ground black pepper	
	chopped fresh parsley, to garnish	

ONE

1. Place the onion, carrot and oil in a bowl. Cover and microwave on HIGH for 1–1½ minutes.

2. Add the wine and bouquet garni. Cover, reduce the power setting and microwave on MEDIUM for 2 minutes.

3. Add the mushrooms, tomatoes and salt and pepper to taste, blending well. Microwave, uncovered, on MEDIUM for 5 minutes, stirring once.

4. Remove and discard the bouquet garni and leave to cool. Garnish with parsley and serve chilled.

TWO

1. Place the onion, carrot and oil in a bowl. Cover and microwave on HIGH for 2–3 minutes.

2. Add the wine and bouquet garni. Cover, reduce the power setting and microwave on MEDIUM for 3½ minutes.

3. Add the mushrooms, tomatoes and salt and pepper to taste, blending well. Microwave, uncovered, on MEDIUM for 8–9 minutes, stirring once.

4. Remove and discard the bouquet garni and leave to cool. Garnish with parsley and serve chilled.

See photograph on page 26-27

SARDINE, AVOCADO AND CORN STARTER

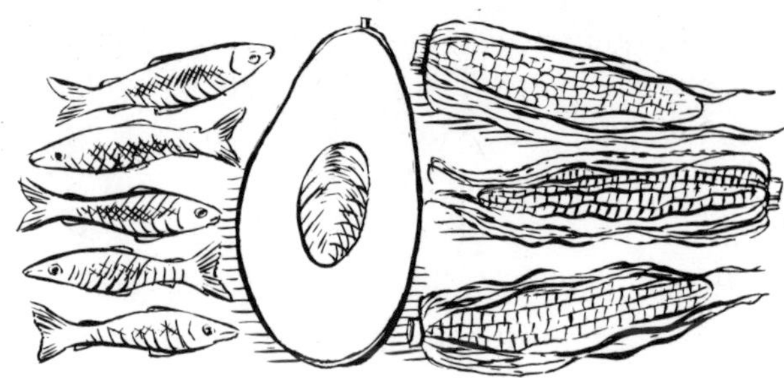

A good economical alternative to a prawn cocktail to start a meal. More of a pâté than a fish cocktail. Serve with fingers of warm wholemeal toast.

ONE		TWO
15 g/½ oz	butter	25 g/1 oz
¼	small onion, peeled and finely chopped	½
1.25 ml/¼ tsp	French mustard	2.5 ml/½ tsp
½ × 125 g/4½ oz	can sardines in oil, drained and bones removed	1 × 125 g/4½ oz
15 ml/1 tbsp	cream cheese	30 ml/2 tbsp
¼	avocado, peeled, stoned and mashed	½
	dash of lemon juice	
	salt and freshly ground black pepper	
75 g/3 oz	canned sweetcorn kernels	175 g/6 oz
	shredded lettuce	
	parsley sprigs, to garnish	

ONE

1. Place the butter and onion in a bowl. Microwave on HIGH for 1 minute. Leave until cold and almost set.

2. Mix the onion butter with the mustard, sardines, cream cheese and avocado, blending well.

3. Add lemon juice and salt and pepper to taste and fold in half of the sweetcorn.

4. Pile onto a bed of shredded lettuce and sprinkle with the remaining sweetcorn. Garnish with sprigs of parsley and serve at once, with wholemeal toast.

TWO

1. Place the butter and onion in a bowl. Microwave on HIGH for 1½ minutes. Leave until cold and almost set.
2. Mix the onion butter with the mustard, sardines, cream cheese and avocado, blending well.
3. Add lemon juice and salt and pepper to taste and fold in half of the sweetcorn.
4. Pile onto a bed of shredded lettuce and sprinkle with the remaining sweetcorn. Garnish with sprigs of parsley and serve at once with wholemeal bread.

ISLE OF SKYE SOUP

Bit of a cheat really but no-one would know that this expensive-tasting mushroom and whisky soup is based on an economical can.

ONE		TWO
1 × 435 g (15 oz)	**small cans creamed mushroom soup**	2 × 435 g (15 oz)
15 ml/1 tbsp	**whisky (Talisker if possible)**	30 ml/2 tbsp
15 ml/1 tbsp	**single cream**	30 ml/2 tbsp
1	**button mushroom, sliced, to garnish (optional)**	2

ONE

1. Place the soup in a bowl. Microwave on HIGH for 2–3 minutes, stirring once.
2. Place the whisky in a soup bowl and pour over the soup.
3. Swirl the cream on top of the soup and garnish with the sliced mushroom. Serve at once.

TWO

1. Place the soup in a bowl. Microwave on HIGH for 3–4 minutes, stirring once.
2. Place the whisky in 2 soup bowls and pour over the soup.
3. Swirl the cream on top of the soup and garnish with the sliced mushrooms. Serve at once.

CRAB AND SWEETCORN SOUP

I first sampled this Chinese style soup as a student when assisting the great authority on Chinese cuisine, Kenneth Lo. I have changed and adapted it many times over the years – here is the tasty microwave version.

ONE		TWO
150 ml/¼ pint	**chicken stock**	300 ml/½ pint
50 g/2 oz	**canned sweetcorn kernels**	100 g/4 oz
25 g/1 oz	**cooked chicken, cut into thin strips**	50 g/2 oz
25 g/1 oz	**canned or fresh crabmeat, flaked**	50 g/2 oz
1.25 ml/¼ tsp	**grated fresh root ginger**	2.5 ml/½ tsp
5 ml/1 tsp	**cornflour**	10 ml/2 tsp
	salt and freshly ground black pepper	
5 ml/1 tsp	**dry sherry**	10 ml/2 tsp
	chopped spring onions, to garnish	

ONE

1. Place the chicken stock, sweetcorn, chicken, crab and ginger in a bowl. Cover and microwave on HIGH for 1½ minutes.
2. Mix the cornflour to a smooth paste with a little water. Stir into the soup with salt and pepper to taste, blending well.
3. Microwave on HIGH for ½–1 minute, stirring twice until clear and thickened.
4. Stir in the sherry and sprinkle with chopped spring onions to garnish. Serve hot.

TWO

1. Place the chicken stock, sweetcorn, chicken, crab and ginger in a bowl. Cover and microwave on HIGH for 3 minutes.
2. Mix the cornflour to a smooth paste with a little water. Stir into the soup with salt and pepper to taste, blending well.
3. Microwave on HIGH for 1–1½ minutes, stirring twice until clear and thickened.
4. Stir in the sherry and sprinkle with chopped spring onions to garnish. Serve hot.

FRESH TOMATO AND HERB SOUP

Without doubt this full-flavoured tomato soup will spoil you to never want a canned variety again – vary the herbs.

ONE		TWO
7 g/¼ oz	**butter**	15 g/½ oz
½	**small onion, peeled and chopped**	1
3.5 ml/¾ tsp	**flour**	7.5 ml/1½ tsp
175 g/6 oz	**tomatoes, skinned, seeded and chopped**	350 g/12 oz
2.5 ml/½ tsp	**chopped fresh mixed herbs**	5 ml/1 tsp
175 ml/6 fl oz	**chicken stock**	350 ml/12 fl oz
5 ml/1 tsp	**tomato purée**	10 ml/2 tsp
1	**bay leaf**	1
	salt and freshly ground black pepper	
10 ml/2 tsp	**milk**	15 ml/1 tbsp
	fresh herbs, to garnish	

ONE

1. Place the butter and onion in a bowl. Cover and microwave on HIGH for 1½ minutes, stirring once.

2. Add the flour, blending well then gradually add the tomatoes, herbs, stock, tomato purée and bay leaf, blending well.

3. Cook, uncovered, on HIGH for 2 minutes, stirring once. Add salt and pepper to taste, blending well. Microwave on HIGH for a further 1–1½ minutes.

4. Remove and discard the bay leaf. Purée the soup in a blender or push through a fine sieve.

5. Stir in the milk and microwave on HIGH for 1½–2 minutes until hot, stirring twice. Serve hot.

TWO

1. Place the butter and onion in a bowl. Cover and microwave on HIGH for 2 minutes, stirring once.

2. Add the flour, blending well then gradually add the tomatoes, herbs, stock, tomato purée and bay leaf, blending well.

3. Cook, uncovered, on HIGH for 4 minutes, stirring once. Add salt and pepper to taste, blending well. Microwave on HIGH for a further 2–3 minutes.

4. Remove and discard the bay leaf. Purée the soup in a blender or push through a fine sieve.

5. Stir in the milk and microwave on HIGH for 3–4 minutes until hot, stirring twice. Serve hot.

CREAMED MUSHROOM AND BACON SOUP

This soup is delicious served with hot butter-flavoured bread – herb or lemon are a good choice.

ONE		TWO
15 g/½ oz	**butter**	25 g/1 oz
50 g/2 oz	**mushrooms, wiped and sliced**	100 g/4 oz
¼	**small onion, peeled and chopped**	½
15 g/½ oz	**flour**	25 g/1 oz
100 ml/4 fl oz	**milk**	200 ml/7 fl oz
75 ml/5 tbsp	**chicken stock**	150 ml/¼ pint
	salt and freshly ground black pepper	
25 g/1 oz	**bacon, rinded**	50 g/2 oz

ONE

1. Place the butter in a bowl and microwave on HIGH for ½ minute to melt. Add the mushrooms and onion, blending well. Cover and cook on HIGH for 1½–2 minutes.

2. Blend the flour with a little of the milk to make a smooth paste. Gradually stir in the remaining milk and stock. Add to the mushroom mixture with salt and pepper to taste, blending well.

3. Microwave on HIGH for 2 minutes, stirring twice.

4. Purée in a blender or push through a fine sieve.

5. Meanwhile place the bacon on a plate and cover with absorbent kitchen towel. Microwave on HIGH for 1–2 minutes until crisp. Allow to cool slightly then crumble coarsely.

6. Reheat the soup on HIGH for 1 minute. Serve hot sprinkled with the crumbled bacon.

TWO

1. Place the butter in a bowl and microwave on HIGH for ¾ minute to melt. Add the mushrooms and onion, blending well. Cover and cook on HIGH for 3–4 minutes.

2. Blend the flour with a little of the milk to make a smooth paste. Gradually stir in the remaining milk and stock. Add to the mushroom mixture with salt and pepper to taste, blending well.

3. Microwave on HIGH for 4 minutes, stirring twice.

4. Purée in a blender or push through a fine sieve.

5. Meanwhile place the bacon on a plate and cover with absorbent kitchen towel. Microwave on HIGH for 2–3 minutes until crisp. Allow to cool slightly then crumble coarsely.

6. Reheat the soup on HIGH for 1½–2 minutes. Serve hot sprinkled with the crumbled bacon.

BRANDIED FRENCH ONION SOUP

It is essential to use a good home-made beef stock in this soup recipe – when in a hurry use canned beef consommé.

ONE		TWO
15 g/½ oz	**butter**	25 g/1 oz
1	**medium onion, peeled and thinly sliced**	2
	pinch of caster sugar	
2.5 ml/½ tsp	**flour**	5 ml/1 tsp
250 ml/9 fl oz	**rich beef stock**	450 ml/¾ pint
	salt and freshly ground black pepper	
1	**slices toasted French bread**	2
25 g/1 oz	**grated cheese**	50 g/2 oz
10 ml/2 tsp	**brandy**	15 ml/1 tbsp

ONE

1. Place the butter in a bowl and microwave on HIGH for ½ minute to melt. Add the onions and microwave, uncovered, on HIGH for 2–2½ minutes, stirring once.

2. Add the sugar, blending well and microwave on HIGH for 1 minute.

3. Add the flour then gradually stir in the stock or beef consommé and salt and pepper to taste. Microwave, uncovered, for 3½ minutes.

4. Meanwhile sprinkle the toast with the cheese.

5. Stir the brandy into the soup, blending well. Pour the soup into a soup bowl, float the cheese slice on top and microwave on HIGH for 1–2 minutes until the soup is hot and the cheese has melted.

TWO

1. Place the butter in a bowl and microwave on HIGH for ¾ minute to melt. Add the onions and microwave, uncovered, on HIGH for 3–4 minutes, stirring once.

2. Add the sugar, blending well and microwave on HIGH for 1½ minutes.

3. Add the flour then gradually stir in the stock or beef consommé and salt and pepper to taste. Microwave, uncovered, for 7 minutes.

4. Meanwhile sprinkle the toast with the cheese.

5. Stir the brandy into the soup, blending well. Pour the soup into two soup bowls, float the cheese slices on top and microwave on HIGH for 2–3 minutes until the soup is hot and the cheese has melted.

STORECUPBOARD STANDBY

This can be easily made on the spur of the moment from a well-stocked storecupboard in half the time it would take to make conventionally.

See photograph on page 25

MINESTRONE WITH PARMESAN

A nourishing and colourful Italian soup.

ONE		TWO
15 g/½ oz	**butter**	25 g/1 oz
40 g/1½ oz	**chopped carrots**	75 g/3 oz
40 g/1½ oz	**chopped celery**	75 g/3 oz
40 g/1½ oz	**diced potato**	75 g/3 oz
½	**small onion, peeled and sliced**	1
½ × 225 g/8 oz	**can tomatoes, drained and chopped**	1 × 225 g/8 oz
15 g/½ oz	**short cut macaroni**	25 g/1 oz
7 g/¼ oz	**flour**	15 g/½ oz
250 ml/9 fl oz	**beef stock**	450 ml/¾ pint
	salt and freshly ground black pepper	
15 ml/1 tbsp	**frozen peas**	30 ml/2 tbsp
	freshly grated Parmesan cheese, to serve	

ONE

1. Place the butter, carrots, celery, potato, onion, tomatoes and macaroni in a bowl. Cover and microwave on HIGH for 3½ minutes.

2. Stir in the flour, blending well. Gradually add the stock and microwave, uncovered, for 3½ minutes.

3. Season to taste with salt and pepper and add the peas. Microwave on HIGH for 1 minute. Cover and leave to stand for 5 minutes. Serve with Parmesan.

TWO

1. Place the butter, carrots, celery, potato, onion, tomatoes and macaroni in a bowl. Cover and microwave on HIGH for 7 minutes.

2. Stir in the flour, blending well. Gradually add the stock and microwave, uncovered, for 7 minutes.

3. Season to taste with salt and pepper and add the peas. Microwave on HIGH for 1½ minutes. Cover and leave to stand for 5 minutes. Serve with Parmesan.

See photograph opposite

SCRAMBLED SMOKED SALMON AND EGGS

There is no need to buy prime smoked salmon for this dish – look out for smoked salmon trimmings at your fishmongers at a fraction of the price. You could also ring the changes by using thin sliced smoked tuna instead.

ONE		TWO
2	**eggs, beaten**	4
7.5 ml/1½ tsp	**single cream**	15 ml/1 tbsp
	salt and freshly ground black pepper	
50 g/2 oz	**smoked salmon, chopped**	100 g/4 oz
7.5 ml/1½ tsp	**snipped fresh parsley or chives**	15 ml/1 tbsp

ONE

1. Mix the eggs with the cream and salt and pepper to taste in a bowl. Microwave on HIGH for 1¾–2 minutes, stirring every ½ minute until just set and creamy.

2. Stir in the smoked salmon pieces and parsley or chives, blending well.

3. Serve at once with brown bread triangles.

TWO

1. Mix the eggs with the cream and salt and pepper to taste in a bowl. Microwave on HIGH for 3 minutes, stirring every ½ minute until just set and creamy.

2. Stir in the smoked salmon pieces and parsley or chives, blending well.

3. Serve at once with drown bread triangles.

Top: Brandied French onion soup (page 23) and Minestrone with Parmesan (this page).

OVERLEAF

From left: Moules marinières (page 30); Leanline chicken and orange pate (page 18); Asparagus eggs (page 29) and Mushrooms à la grecque (page 20).

SAVOURY BAKED EGGS

Eggs baked with cream and pâté make a delicious starter to serve with hot toast fingers. Cook on DEFROST power to ensure that the egg is just lightly set.

ONE		TWO
25 g/1 oz	**smooth spreading pâté**	50 g/2 oz
1	**large eggs**	2
30 ml/2 tbsp	**double cream**	60 ml/4 tbsp
	salt and freshly ground black pepper	
	parsley sprigs, to garnish	

ONE

1. Spread the pâté over the base of a lightly greased ramekin dish.
2. Crack the egg over the pâté and carefully puncture the yolk with the tip of a knife.
3. Spoon over the cream and season to taste with salt and pepper.
4. Cover loosely with cling film and microwave on DEFROST for 3–3½ minutes until the egg is just set.
5. Garnish with parsley sprigs and serve at once with hot toast fingers.

TWO

1. Spread the pâté over the base of 2 lightly greased ramekin dishes.
2. Crack the eggs over the pâté and carefully puncture the yolks with the tip of a knife.
3. Spoon over the cream and season to taste with salt and pepper.
4. Cover loosely with cling film and microwave on DEFROST for 5–7 minutes until the eggs are just set.
5. Garnish with parsley sprigs and serve at once with hot toast fingers.

Monkfish and prawn brochettes (page 40) and Creamy seafood pasta (page 43).

ASPARAGUS EGGS

Asparagus makes an elegant entrance into this delightfully creamy egg starter. Use green rather than white asparagus for colour.

ONE		TWO
2	**eggs, beaten**	4
7.5 ml/1½ tsp	**milk**	15 ml/1 tbsp
	salt and freshly ground black pepper	
15 g/½ oz	**butter**	25 g/1 oz
3	**cooked asparagus tips, chopped**	6
7.5 ml/1½ tsp	**snipped chives**	15 ml/1 tbsp

ONE

1. Mix the eggs with the milk and salt and pepper to taste in a bowl. Microwave on HIGH for 1¾–2 minutes, stirring every ½ minute until just set and creamy.
2. Stir in the asparagus and chives, blending well.
3. Serve at once with wholemeal toast fingers, if liked.

TWO

1. Mix the eggs with the milk and salt and pepper to taste in a bowl. Microwave on HIGH for 3 minutes, stirring every ½ minute until just set and creamy.
2. Stir in the asparagus and chives, blending well.
3. Serve at once with wholemeal toast fingers, if liked.

See photograph on page 26-27

MOULES MARINIÈRE

Delicious and elegant, mussels make succulent eating when cooked the microwave way. Tightly covered and steamed in a little wine they retain their unique delicate flavour and texture.

ONE		TWO
300 ml/½ pint	**mussels**	600 ml/1 pint
15 g/½ oz	**butter**	25 g/1 oz
½	**small onion, peeled and finely chopped**	1
½	**garlic clove, peeled and crushed**	1
75 ml/5 tbsp	**dry white wine**	150 ml/¼ pint
	freshly ground black pepper	
	chopped fresh parsley, to garnish	

ONE

1. Wash and scrub the mussels removing the beards. Discard any mussels that are open.

2. Place the butter, onion and garlic in a bowl and microwave on HIGH for 1½ minutes, stirring once.

3. Add the wine and pepper to taste, blending well. Microwave on HIGH until the mixture boils, about 1½ minutes.

4. Add the mussels, cover and microwave on HIGH for 1½–2 minutes or until the shells open. Discard any mussels whose shells do not open.

5. Transfer to a serving dish, garnish with parsley and serve immediately.

TWO

1. Wash and scrub the mussels removing the beards. Discard any mussels that are open.

2. Place the butter, onion and garlic in a bowl and microwave on HIGH for 2½ minutes, stirring once.

3. Add the wine and pepper to taste, blending well. Microwave on HIGH until the mixture boils about 2½ minutes.

4. Add the mussels, cover and microwave on HIGH f r 3–3½ minutes or until the shells open. Discard any mussels whose shells do not open.

5. Transfer to a serving dish, garnish with parsley. Serve at once.

See photograph on page 26·27

PASTA WITH CREAM AND PARMESAN

A classic pasta starter that is quick and easy to make. Double the portions and add chopped ham or tuna fish for a main course.

ONE		TWO
50 g/2 oz	**dried pasta quills**	100 g /4 oz
300 ml/½ pint	**boiling chicken stock or water**	450 ml/¾ pint
7 g/¼ oz	**butter**	15 g/½ oz
75 ml/5 tbsp	**double cream**	150 ml/¼ pint
	salt and freshly ground black pepper	
10 ml/2 tsp	**grated Parmesan cheese**	20 ml/4 tsp
	pinch of sweet paprika	

ONE

1. Place the pasta in a deep bowl with the boiling stock. Cover and microwave on HIGH for 12–14 minutes then allow to stand for 5–10 minutes.

2. While the pasta is standing, place the butter, cream and salt and pepper to taste in a bowl. Microwave on HIGH for 1 minute until hot, stirring once.

3. Drain the cooked pasta and place on a serving plate. Spoon over the cream sauce and toss gently together to mix.

4. Sprinkle with the Parmesan cheese and paprika and serve at once.

TWO

1. Place the pasta in a deep bowl with the boiling stock. Cover and microwave on HIGH for 12–14 minutes then allow to stand for 5–10 minutes.

2. While the pasta is standing, place the butter, cream and salt and pepper to taste in a bowl. Microwave on HIGH for 1–1½ minutes until hot, stirring once.

3. Drain the cooked pasta and place on a serving plate. Spoon over the cream sauce and toss gently together to mix.

4. Sprinkle with the Parmesan cheese and paprika and serve at once.

STORECUPBOARD STANDBY

Pasta with Cream and Parmesan can easily be made on the spur of the moment from a well-stocked storecupboard and refrigerator.

BLUSHING BAKED GRAPEFRUIT

Pink grapefruit topped with a little redcurrant jelly is perhaps the speediest of all microwave starters.

ONE		TWO
1	**pink grapefruit halves**	2
5 ml/1 tsp	**redcurrant jelly**	10 ml/2 tsp

ONE

1. Carefully cut around and loosen the grapefruit segments with a grapefruit knife or sharp knife.

2. Spread the jelly over the cut grapefruit surface. Place on a serving dish and microwave on HIGH for 1–1¼ minutes. Serve at once.

TWO

1. Carefully cut around and loosen the grapefruit segments with a grapefruit knife or sharp knife.

2. Spread the jelly over the cut grapefruit surface. Place on a serving dish and microwave on HIGH for 2–2½ minutes. Serve at once.

BLT's

BLT's – American for bacon, lettuce and tomato sandwiches – are fast food favourites with a difference, as they provide a balanced nutritional meal.

ONE		TWO
3	**rashers streaky bacon, rinded**	6
2	**slices wholemeal bread**	4
15 ml/1 tbsp	**mayonnaise**	30 ml/2 tbsp
	few crisp lettuce leaves	
1	**tomatoes, sliced**	2

ONE

1. Place the bacon on a plate and cover with a sheet of absorbent kitchen towel. Microwave on HIGH for 2–3 minutes or until crisp and cooked.

2. Spread one slice of bread with some of the mayonnaise. Cover with the lettuce leaves and sliced tomato.

3. Top with the cooked bacon and any remaining mayonnaise. Cover with the remaining bread. Cut into triangles and serve at once.

TWO

1. Place the bacon on a plate and cover with a sheet of absorbent kitchen towel. Microwave on HIGH for 3½–4 minutes or until crisp and cooked.

2. Spread two slices of bread with some of the mayonnaise. Cover with the lettuce leaves and sliced tomato.

3. Top with the cooked bacon and any remaining mayonnaise. Cover with the remaining bread. Cut into triangles and serve at once.

POTTED CHICKEN AND TONGUE

A quick visit to the delicatessen counter of your local supermarket will provide all the basic ingredients you need.

ONE		TWO
15 g/½ oz	**butter**	25 g/1 oz
¼	**small onion, peeled and finely chopped**	½
75 g/3 oz	**cooked chicken, skinned and finely chopped**	175 g/6 oz
25 g/1 oz	**cooked tongue, finely chopped**	40 g/1½ oz
7.5 ml/1½ tsp	**dry sherry**	15 ml/1 tbsp
	salt and freshly ground black pepper	
	Topping:	
20 g/¾ oz	**butter**	40 g/1½ oz
	bay leaves	

ONE

1. Place the butter and onion in a bowl and microwave on HIGH for 1–1½ minutes, stirring once.
2. Add the chicken, tongue, sherry and salt and pepper to taste, blending well. Spoon into a small terrine or serving dish and press down well.
3. Place the butter for the topping in a bowl and microwave on HIGH for ¾ minute to melt.
4. Pour over the potted mixture. Arrange a few bay leaves attractively on top and chill until set.
5. Serve straight from the dish with fingers of toast.

TWO

1. Place the butter and onion in a bowl and microwave on HIGH for 2 minutes, stirring once.
2. Add the chicken, tongue, sherry and salt and pepper to taste, blending well. Spoon into a small terrine or serving dish and press down well.
3. Place the butter for the topping in a bowl and microwave on HIGH for 1 minute to melt.
4. Pour over the potted mixture. Arrange a few bay leaves attractively on top and chill to set.
5. Serve straight from the dish with fingers of toast.

PIPERANDA

Piperanda is rather like the classic French egg and tomato dish pipérade but is made with ham and peppers too. Serve with toast fingers or crusty Farmhouse bread wedges.

ONE		TWO
20 g/¾ oz	**butter**	40 g/1½ oz
½	**small onion, peeled and chopped**	1
½	**small green pepper, cored, seeded and finely chopped**	1
25 g/1 oz	**tomatoes, chopped**	50 g/2 oz
25 g/1 oz	**cooked ham, chopped**	50 g/2 oz
2	**small eggs, beaten**	4
	salt and freshly ground black pepper	
	parsley sprigs, to garnish	

ONE

1. Place the butter, onion and pepper in a bowl. Cover and microwave on HIGH for 1–2 minutes, stirring once.
2. Add the tomatoes, ham, eggs and salt and pepper to taste, blending well. Microwave, uncovered, on HIGH for 2–2½ minutes, stirring ever ½ minute until lightly scrambled, creamy, and just set.
3. Garnish with parsley sprigs and serve at once.

TWO

1. Place the butter, onion and pepper in a bowl. Cover and microwave on HIGH for 2–2½ minutes, stirring once.
2. Add the tomatoes, ham, eggs and salt and pepper to taste, blending well. Microwave, uncovered, on HIGH for 3–4 minutes, stirring every ½ minute until lightly scrambled, creamy and just set.
3. Garnish with parsley sprigs and serve at once.

COOK'S TIP

Piperanda is a good, quick spur of the moment dish to use up leftover cooked ham.

OMELETTE FINES HERBES

Eggs cook amazingly fast in the microwave so it is important to judge the cooking time carefully when making this omelette. Err on the side of safety by undercooking and allowing a generous standing time.

ONE		TWO
2	**eggs, beaten**	4
20 ml/4 tsp	**milk**	45 ml/3 tbsp
	salt and freshly ground black pepper	
7 g/¼ oz	**butter**	15 g/½ oz
15 ml/1 tbsp	**chopped fresh mixed herbs**	30 ml/2 tbsp

ONE

1. Mix the eggs with the milk and salt and pepper to taste, blending well.

2. Place the butter in a 15–18 cm/6–7 inch pie plate and microwave on HIGH for ½ minute. Swirl the butter over the plate to coat.

3. Pour in the egg mixture, cover with pierced cling film and microwave on HIGH for ¾ minute. Using a fork, move the cooked egg from the edge of the dish to the centre. Re-cover and microwave on HIGH for a further ½–1 minute. Allow to stand for 2 minutes to finish cooking.

4. Loosen the omelette with a spatula, sprinkle with half of the herbs and fold in half to serve. Serve sprinkled with the remaining herbs.

TWO

1. Mix the eggs with the milk and salt and pepper to taste, blending well.

2. Place the butter in a 25 cm/10 inch pie plate and microwave on HIGH for ½–¾ minute. Swirl the butter over the plate to coat.

3. Pour in the egg mixture, cover with pierced cling film and microwave on HIGH for 1¼–1½ minutes. Using a fork, move the cooked egg from the edge of the dish to the centre. Re-cover and microwave on HIGH for a further 1¼–1½ minutes. Allow to stand for 2 minutes to finish cooking.

4. Loosen the omelette with a spatula, sprinkle with half of the herbs and fold in half to serve. Serve sprinkled with the remaining herbs.

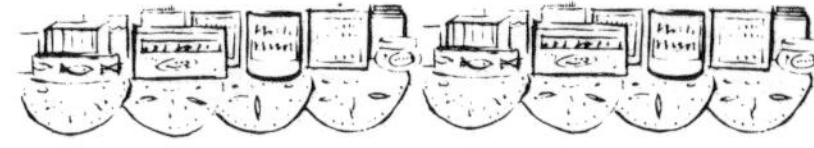

STORECUPBOARD STANDBY

Another storecupboard favourite, try using grated cheese or chopped tomatoes instead of herbs.

BACON AND EGGS

Crisp bacon and lightly baked eggs with a tomato garnish make delicious eating at any time of the day – breakfast, brunch, lunch or supper time. Serve with toast for a speedy feast.

ONE		TWO
2	**rashers bacon, rinded**	4
1	**tomatoes, halved**	2
1	**eggs**	2

ONE

1. Place the bacon on a plate and microwave on HIGH for ½ minute. Add the tomato halves, cut sides up.

2. Break the egg into a small lightly greased ramekin dish or cup and puncture the yolk with the tip of a knife. Cover loosely with cling film and place on the plate.

3. Microwave on HIGH for 1½ minutes then loosen the egg from the dish and slide onto the plate to serve.

TWO

1. Divide he bacon between two plates and microwave on HIGH for 1 minute. Add the tomato halves, cut sides up.

2. Break the eggs into two small lightly greased ramekin dishes or cups and puncture the yolks with the tip of a knife. Cover loosely with cling film and place on the plates.

3. Microwave on HIGH for 2½–3 minutes. Leave to stand for ½ minute then loosen the eggs from the dishes and slide onto the plates to serve.

CROQUE MONSIEUR

This classic French sandwich is usually pan fried in butter. Here is a simple way to prepare it in the microwave using a browning dish. Serve hot with a crunchy green salad.

ONE		TWO
2	**small slices thin white bread, crusts removed**	4
	made mustard	
1	**slices Gruyère cheese**	2
1	**slices cooked ham**	2
15 g/½ oz	**butter**	25 g/1 oz

ONE

1. Spread one slice of bread with mustard to taste. Top with the cheese and the ham. Cover with the remaining slice of bread and press down well to seal.

2. Place the butter in a bowl and microwave on HIGH for ¼ minute to melt.

3. Preheat a browning dish on HIGH for 8 minutes or according to the manufacturer's instructions.

4. Brush one side of the sandwich with the melted butter. Place in the browning dish, buttered side down, and cook for 1–2 minutes until golden brown on the underside. Quickly brush the second side with melted butter, turn over and microwave on HIGH for ½–1 minute until hot.

5. Cut the sandwich in half and serve at once with a green salad.

TWO

1. Spread half of the bread slices with mustard to taste. Top with the cheese and the ham. Cover with the remaining slice of bread and press down well to seal.

2. Place the butter in a bowl and microwave on HIGH for ½ minute to melt.

3. Preheat a browning dish on HIGH for 8 minutes or according to the manufacturer's instructions.

4. Brush one side of each sandwich with the melted butter. Place in the browning dish, buttered side down, and cook on for 1–2 minutes until golden brown on the underside. Quickly brush the second sides with melted butter, turn over and microwave on HIGH for 1–1½ minutes until hot.

5. Cut each sandwich in half and serve at once with a green salad.

CREAMY CHEESE AND ALE

An old English recipe that adapts well for cooking in the microwave. Take care not to overcook or the cheese will become stringy and tough.

ONE		TWO
50 g/2 oz	**Cheshire cheese**	100 g/4 oz
2.5 ml/½ tsp	**made mustard**	5 ml/1 tsp
15–30 ml/1–2 tbsp	**ale**	45–60 ml/3–4 tbsp
1	**slices hot buttered toast**	2

ONE

1. Cut the cheese into very thin slices and spread with the mustard. Place in a small shallow dish and pour over the ale.

2. Microwave on DEFROST for 2–3 minutes until smooth and creamy, stirring twice.

3. Spread on the toast and serve at once.

TWO

1. Cut the cheese into very thin slices and spread with the mustard. Place in a small shallow dish and

pour over the ale.

2. Microwave on DEFROST for 4–5 minutes until smooth and creamy, stirring twice.

3. Spread on the toast and serve at once.

SAVE AND SAVOUR

Creamy Cheese and Ale can be made using any kind of leftover cheese. If you don't have ale in the cupboard, use milk instead.

CORNED WELSH RAREBIT

Welsh rarebit is a time-honoured favourite snack – here it is made more substantial with the addition of corned beef.

ONE		TWO
1	**slices toasted bread**	2
15 g/½ oz	**butter**	25 g/1 oz
1	**slices corned beef**	2
50 g/2 oz	**grated cheese**	100 g/4 oz
	few drops Worcestershire sauce	
	salt and freshly ground black pepper	

ONE

1. Spread the toast with the butter. Cover with the corned beef.

2. Mix the cheese with the Worcestershire sauce and salt and pepper to taste, blending well. Pile on top of the corned beef.

3. Microwave on HIGH for ¾ minute or until the cheese has melted. Serve at once.

TWO

1. Spread the toast with the butter. Cover with the corned beef.

2. Mix the cheese with the Worcestershire sauce and salt and pepper to taste, blending well. Pile on top of the corned beef.

3. Microwave on HIGH for 1½ minutes or until the cheese has melted. Serve at once.

MACARONI CHEESE

A storecupboard favourite. The mornay sauce can be made with any kind of cheese from an everyday Cheddar to an exotic smoked cheese with ham.

ONE		TWO
50 g/2 oz	**macaroni**	100 g/4 oz
300 ml/½ pint	**boiling water**	450 ml/¾ pint
150 ml/¼ pint	**hot Mornay Sauce (see page 96)**	300 ml/½ pint
1	**small tomatoes, sliced**	2
	chopped fresh parsley to garnish	

ONE

1. Place the macaroni in a large bowl with the water. Cover and microwave on HIGH for 10 minutes, stirring once. Leave to stand, covered for 5 minutes then drain thoroughly.

2. Mix the macaroni with the Mornay Sauce and place in a serving dish.

3. Top with the sliced tomato and microwave on HIGH for 1½ minutes. Sprinkle with chopped parsley and serve at once.

TWO

1. Place the macaroni in a large bowl with the water. Cover and microwave on HIGH for 10 minutes, stirring once. Leave to stand, covered for 5 minutes then drain thoroughly.

2. Mix the macaroni with the Mornay Sauce and place in a serving dish.

3. Top with the sliced tomato and microwave on HIGH for 2–3 minutes. Sprinkle with chopped parsley and serve at once.

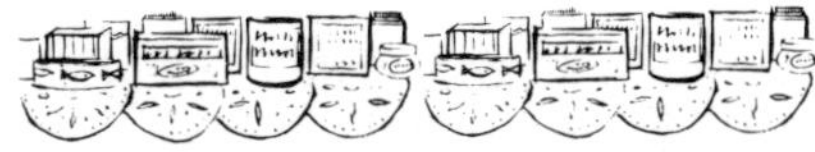

STORECUPBOARD STANDBY

Macaroni cheese is a nourishing dish using simple storecupboard ingredients.

WHOLEMEAL MUFFIN PIZZAS

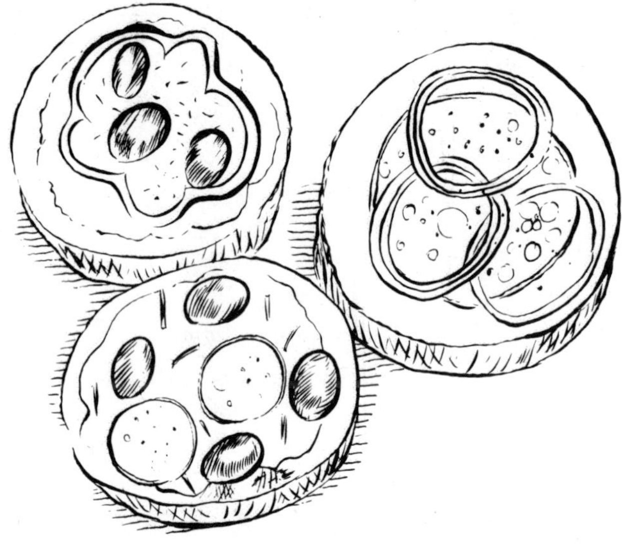

Ordinary pizzas with their yeasted bread dough base really do seem too much effort for 1 or 2 – here is a good satisfying compromise, tasty home-made pizzas made with wholemeal muffins. They really do taste so good it is worth making double portions to freeze.

ONE		TWO
50 g/2 oz	**drained canned tomatoes**	100 g/4 oz
5 ml/1 tsp	**tomato purée**	10 ml/2 tsp
½	**small onion, peeled and finely chopped**	1
	pinch of dried oregano	
	pinch of dried basil	
1	**wholemeal muffins, split**	2
15 g/½ oz	**sliced salami, pepperoni or garlic sausage**	25 g/1 oz
2	**pimiento-stuffed olives, sliced**	4
40 g/1½ oz	**Mozzarella cheese, grated**	75 g/3 oz

ONE

1. Place the tomatoes, tomato purée, onion and herbs in a bowl. Cover and microwave on HIGH for 1½ – 2 minutes until thick and pulpy, stirring once. Leave to cool.

2. Spread the tomato mixture on top of the muffin halves. Top with the sliced sausage, olives and cheese.

3. Microwave on HIGH for ¾–1¼ minutes. Serve at once.

TWO

1. Place the tomatoes, tomato purée, onion and herbs in a bowl. Cover and microwave on HIGH for 3–4 minutes until thick and pulpy, stirring once. Leave to cool.

2. Spread the tomato mixture on top of the muffin halves. Top with the sliced sausage, olives and cheese.

3. Microwave on HIGH for 2–2½ minutes. Serve at once.

FREEZABILITY

Wholemeal muffin pizzas will freeze well for up to 2 months. Cook from frozen, 2 muffin pizza halves to serve 1 should be cooked on HIGH for 1½–2 minutes; 4 muffin pizza halves to serve 2 should be cooked on HIGH for 4–4½ minutes.

POP ALONG PIZZA

A speedy pizza made with a quick scone dough rather than a time-consuming bread dough.

ONE		TWO
4	**rashers streaky bacon, rinded**	8
25 g/1 oz	**butter**	50 g/2 oz
½	**small onion, peeled and chopped**	1
100 g/4 oz	**drained canned tomatoes**	225 g/8 oz
	pinch of dried mixed herbs	
	salt and freshly ground black pepper	
50 g/2 oz	**self-raising flour**	100 g/4 oz
	water to mix	
7.5 ml/1½ tsp	**oil**	15 ml/1 tbsp
50 g/2 oz	**Mozzarella cheese, sliced**	100 g/4 oz
	few green or black olives, to garnish	

ONE

1. Place the bacon on a plate, cover with a sheet of absorbent kitchen towel and microwave on HIGH for about 2 minutes until crisp.

2. Place half the butter in a bowl with the onion. Microwave on HIGH for 1½–2 minutes until soft. Add the tomatoes, herbs and salt and pepper to taste, blending well. Cover and microwave on HIGH for 2–2½ minutes, stirring once.

3. To make the pizza base, rub the remaining butter into the flour and add 1–2 tablespoons water to make a soft dough. Knead lightly until smooth then roll out on a lightly floured surface to a 13 cm/5 inch round.

4. Preheat a browning dish on HIGH for 8 minutes or according to the manufacturer's instructions. Brush with the oil, add the dough and top with the tomato and herb mixture, spreading it evenly over the dough surface. Place the cheese on top and microwave on HIGH for about 2–3 minutes until bubbling and melted.

5. Place the bacon on the pizza to make a lattice and garnish with a few olives. Microwave on HIGH for ½ minute to reheat.

6. Serve straight from the dish.

TWO

1. Place the bacon on a plate, cover with a sheet of absorbent kitchen towel and microwave on HIGH for about 3¼–4 minutes until crisp.

2. Place half the butter in a bowl with the onion. Microwave on HIGH for 2½–3 minutes until soft. Add the tomatoes, herbs and salt and pepper to taste, blending well. Cover and microwave on HIGH for 4 minutes, stirring once.

3. To make the pizza base, rub the remaining butter into the flour and add 3–4 tablespoons water to make a soft dough. Knead lightly until smooth then roll out on a lightly floured surface to a 18 cm/7 inch round.

4. Preheat a browning dish on HIGH for 8 minutes or according to the manufacturer's instructions. Brush with the oil, add the dough and top with the tomato and herb mixture spreading it evenly over the dough surface. Place the cheese on top and microwave on HIGH for about 5½ minutes until bubbling and melted.

5. Place the bacon on the pizza to make a lattice and garnish with a few olives. Microwave on HIGH for ½ minute to reheat.

6. Serve straight from the dish.

COTTAGE CHEESE AND RAISIN BAKED POTATO

Potatoes cooked in their jackets in the microwave are not as crisp as the traditional oven-baked kind. Wrapping in absorbent kitchen towel does however give a drier and crisper finish.

ONE		TWO
one 175 g/6 oz	**potatoes, scrubbed**	two 175 g/6 oz
50 g/2 oz	**cottage cheese**	100 g/4 oz
25 g/1 oz	**raisins**	50 g/2 oz
15 ml/1 tbsp	**unsweetened orange juice**	30 ml/2 tbsp
½	**stick celery, scrubbed and chopped**	1
	salt and freshly ground black pepper	
	thin slices of orange, to garnish	

ONE

1. Prick the potato thoroughly and wrap in a double thickness of absorbent kitchen towel. Microwave on HIGH for 4–6 minutes, turning over once. Leave to stand for 3–4 minutes to soften.

2. Cut the potato in half and remove the flesh. Mash in a bowl with the cottage cheese, raisins, orange juice, celery and salt and pepper to taste, blending well.

3. Pile the mixture back into the potato skins. Microwave on HIGH for 1 minute to reheat, garnish with thin slices of orange and serve at once.

TWO

1. Prick the potatoes thoroughly and wrap in or place on a double thickness piece of absorbent kitchen towel. Microwave on HIGH for 6–8 minutes, turning over once. Leave to stand for 3–4 minutes to soften.

2. Cut the potatoes in half and remove the flesh. Mash in a bowl with the cottage cheese, raisins, orange juice, celery and salt and pepper to taste, blending well.

3. Pile the mixture back into the potato skins. Microwave on HIGH for 1½ minutes to reheat, garnish with thin slices of orange and serve at once.

JACKET SPECIALS

Jacket potatoes make warming, highly nutritious snack and supper dishes. Use good fluffy potatoes such as King Edwards or Maris Piper for the best result.

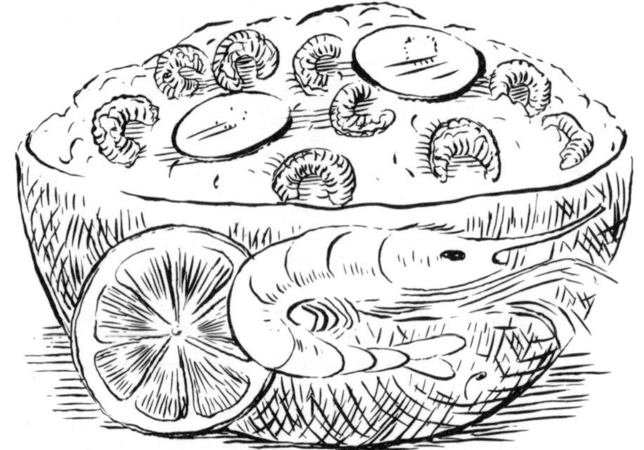

ONE		TWO
1 × 225 g/8 oz	**potatoes, scrubbed**	2 × 225 g/8 oz
	Corned Beef Hash Filling:	
15 g/½ oz	**savoury butter with black pepper**	25 g/1 oz
25 g/1 oz	**corned beef, chopped**	50 g/2 oz
5 ml/1 tsp	**sweet pickle**	10 ml/2 tsp
	tomato and cucumber slices, to garnish	
	Lemon Prawn Filling:	
15 g/½ oz	**savoury butter with lemon and parsley**	25 g/1 oz
25 g/1 oz	**peeled prawns**	50 g/2 oz
	lemon slices, to garnish	

ONE

1. Prick the potato and wrap in a sheet of absorbent kitchen towel. Microwave on HIGH for 4–6 minutes, turning over once. Leave to stand for 3–4 minutes to soften.

2. Split the potato in half and scoop out the flesh into a bowl.

3. To fill with corned beef hash mixture, mash the potato with the butter. Stir in the corned beef and pickle, blending well. Spoon back into the potato shells.

4. To fill with lemon prawn mixture, mash the potato with the butter. Stir in the prawns, blending well. Spoon back into the potato shells.

5. Microwave on HIGH for 1 minute to reheat. Garnish and serve at once.

TWO

1. Prick the potatoes and wrap in a sheet of absorbent kitchen towel. Microwave on HIGH for 6–8 minutes, turning over once. Leave to stand for 3–4 minutes to soften.

2. Split the potatoes in half and scoop out the flesh into a bowl.

3. To fill with corned beef hash mixture, mash the potato with the butter. Stir in the corned beef and pickle, blending well. Spoon back into the potato shells.

4. To fill with lemon prawn mixture, mash the potato with the butter. Stir in the prawns, blending well. Spoon back into the potato shells.

5. Microwave on HIGH for 1½ minutes to reheat. Garnish and serve at once.

BEAN AND SAUSAGE SLOPPY JOES

These hearty snack 'sandwiches' are best served with a knife and fork or at the very least a large paper napkin.

ONE		TWO
50 g/2 oz	**minced beef**	100 g/4 oz
¼	**small green pepper, cored, seeded and chopped**	½
¼	**onion, peeled and chopped**	½
75 g/3 oz	**canned baked beans and sausages**	175 g/6 oz
15 ml/1 tbsp	**tomato ketchup**	30 ml/2 tbsp
	salt	
	pinch of chilli powder	
1	**long crusty rolls**	2
1	**lettuce leaves**	2

ONE

1. Place the beef, pepper and onion in a bowl. Microwave on HIGH for 4 minutes, stirring twice.

2. Stir in the beans and sausages, ketchup, salt and chilli powder, blending well. Reduce the power setting and microwave on MEDIUM for 6 minutes, stirring twice.

3. Halve the roll lengthways. Place the lettuce leaf on the base of the roll, cover with the meat mixture and finally the bread roll top. Serve at once.

TWO

1. Place the beef, pepper and onion in a bowl. Microwave on HIGH for 7–8 minutes, stirring twice.

2. Stir in the beans and sausages, ketchup, salt and chilli powder, blending well. Reduce the power setting and microwave on MEDIUM for 10 minutes, stirring twice.

3. Halve the rolls lengthways. Place a lettuce leaf on the base of each roll, cover with the meat mixture and finally the bread roll tops. Serve at once.

SPICY PITTA POCKETS

Plain or wholemeal pitta breads make ideal 'pockets' for holding savoury mixtures. In this recipe they are stuffed with a spicy curried mixture to make a sandwich with a difference.

ONE		TWO
75 g/3 oz	**lean minced beef**	175 g/6 oz
¼	**small onion, peeled and chopped**	½
¼	**green dessert apple, cored and chopped**	½
7 g/¼ oz	**raisins**	15 g/½ oz
1.25 ml/¼ tsp	**curry powder**	2.5 ml/½ tsp
	salt and freshly ground black pepper	
½	**pitta bread**	1
15 ml/1 tbsp	**natural yogurt**	30 ml/2 tbsp
	pinch of garam masala	

ONE

1. Place the beef and onion in a bowl and microwave on HIGH for 2–3 minutes until cooked, stirring twice to break up any large lumps of mince.

2. Drain off any excess fat then add the apple, raisins, curry powder and salt and pepper to taste, blending well.

3. Cover and microwave on HIGH for 1–2 minutes until the apple is tender.

4. Carefully cut the pitta bread in half with a sharp knife to make a pocket.

5. Fill with the savoury curried beef mixture and top with the yogurt. Serve at once.

TWO

1. Place the beef and onion in a bowl and microwave on HIGH for 4–4½ minutes until cooked, stirring twice to break up any large lumps of mince.

2. Drain away any excess fat and add the apple, raisins, curry powder and salt and pepper to taste, blending well.

3. Cover and microwave on HIGH for 2–3 minutes until the apple is tender.

4. Using a sharp knife halve the pitta bread crossways then carefully cut between the halves to make two pockets.

5. Fill with the savoury curried beef mixture and top with the yogurt. Serve at once.

Main Meals

MONKFISH AND PRAWN BROCHETTES

Monkfish is a deep sea fish which has such an ugly head that usually only the tail is sold. Its flesh is firm, white and very succulent and makes a perfect partner to pink prawns in these delicious brochettes.

ONE		TWO
225 g/8 oz	**monkfish tails**	450 g/1 lb
4	**large Mediterranean prawns, peeled**	8
2	**bay leaves**	4
15 ml/1 tbsp	**olive oil**	30 ml/2 tbsp
	freshly ground white pepper	
1	**recipe hot Hollandaise Sauce, to serve (see page 97)**	1

ONE

1. Skin the monkfish, then remove the flesh from either side of the central bone. Cut into bite-sized chunks.

2. Thread onto a short wooden skewer, alternating with the prawns and bay leaves. Brush with the olive oil and season with pepper to taste.

3. Cover loosely with cling film and microwave on HIGH for 2½–3 minutes until the monkfish is opaque and flakes easily when tested with a fork. Serve with hot Hollandaise sauce (see page 97).

TWO

1. Skin the monkfish, then remove the flesh from either side of the central bone. Cut into bite-sized chunks.

2. Thread onto two short wooden skewers, alternating with the prawns and bay leaves. Brush with the olive oil and season with pepper to taste.

3. Cover loosely with cling film and microwave on HIGH for 5–7 minutes until the monkfish is opaque

and flakes easily when tested with a fork. Serve with hot Hollandaise sauce (see page 97).

See photograph on page 28

FRAGRANT SEAFOOD PAELLA

This Spanish speciality relies upon saffron strands for its fragrant aroma and flavour. If unavailable use a little ground turmeric instead to achieve the same golden yellow rice but not the same flavour.

ONE		TWO
7.5 ml/1½ tsp	**olive oil**	15 ml/1 tbsp
½	**small onion, peeled and chopped**	1
½	**garlic clove, peeled and crushed**	1
75 g/3 oz	**long grain rice**	175 g/6 oz
175 ml/6 fl oz	**boiling chicken stock**	350 ml/12 fl oz
	pinch of saffron strands	
	salt and freshly ground black pepper	
25 g/1 oz	**frozen peas**	50 g/2 oz
5	**mussels cooked then left on their half shells**	10
50 g/2 oz	**cooked chicken, skinned and chopped**	100 g/4 oz
4	**whole prawns**	8
25 g/1 oz	**hot spicy sausage, diced**	50 g/2 oz

ONE

1. Place the oil, onion and garlic in a large bowl. Cover and microwave on HIGH for 1½–2 minutes.

2. Stir in the rice, stock, saffron strands and salt and pepper to taste, blending well. Cover and microwave on HIGH for 3 minutes. Reduce the power setting and microwave on MEDIUM for a further 10 minutes, stirring twice. Leave to stand, covered, for 5 minutes or until the rice is tender and the liquid absorbed.

3. Add the peas, mussels, chicken, prawns and sausage, tossing lightly to mix. Cover and microwave on HIGH for 2–3 minutes to reheat. Serve at once.

TWO

1. Place the oil, onion and garlic in a large bowl. Cover and microwave on HIGH for 3–4 minutes.

2. Stir in the rice, stock, saffron strands and salt and pepper to taste, blending well. Cover and microwave on HIGH for 3 minutes. Reduce the power setting and microwave on MEDIUM for a further 10 minutes, stirring twice. Leave to stand, covered, for 5 minutes or until the rice is tender and the liquid absorbed.

3. Add the peas, mussels, chicken, prawns and sausage, tossing lightly to mix. Cover and microwave on HIGH for 3–4 minutes to reheat. Serve at once.

CHIVE FISH BAKE

Quick mid-week meals need not be complicated or repetitive – here is a deliciously easy recipe which is perfect for a weekday supper.

ONE		TWO
one 175 g/6 oz	**pieces of cod or haddock fillet**	two 175 g/6 oz
5 ml/1 tsp	**chive mustard**	10 ml/2 tsp
25 g/1 oz	**Cheddar cheese, grated**	50 g/2 oz
1	**tomatoes, sliced**	2

ONE

1. Place the fish in a small shallow dish. Spread with the chive mustard and sprinkle with the cheese. Arrange the tomato slices over the top.

2. Cover and microwave on HIGH for 3–4 minutes or until the fish is opaque and flakes easily when tested with a fork.

3. Serve at once with vegetables in season.

TWO

1. Place the fish in a small shallow dish. Spread with the chive mustard and sprinkle with the cheese. Arrange the tomato slices over the top.

2. Cover and microwave on HIGH for 5–6 minutes or until the fish is opaque and flakes easily when tested with a fork.

3. Serve at once with vegetables in season.

SEAFOOD AND FISH PIE

Chunks of white fish and prawns topped with fluffy potato make a welcome change to the usual mid-week cottage pie.

ONE		TWO
100 g/4 oz	**cooked white fish, flaked into chunks**	225 g/8 oz
50 g/2 oz	**peeled prawns**	100 g/4 oz
150 ml/¼ pint	**hot Basic White or Parsley Sauce (see page 95)**	300 ml/½ pint
200 g/7 oz	**potatoes, peeled and cubed**	400 g/14 oz
15 ml/1 tbsp	**water**	30 ml/2 tbsp
15 g/½ oz	**butter**	25 g/1 oz
	salt and freshly ground black pepper	

ONE

1. Mix the fish with the prawns and sauce in a small ovenproof dish.

2. Place the potato and water in a bowl. Cover and microwave on HIGH for 4–5 minutes until tender. Drain and mash with the butter and salt and pepper to taste. Pipe or spoon over the fish mixture to cover.

3. Microwave on HIGH for 2 minutes to reheat then brown under a preheated grill, if liked.

TWO

1. Mix the fish with the prawns and sauce in a small ovenproof dish.

2. Place the potato and water in a bowl. Cover and microwave on HIGH for 8–10 minutes until tender. Drain and mash with the butter and salt and pepper to taste. Pipe or spoon over the fish mixture to cover.

3. Microwave on HIGH for 4 minutes to reheat then brown under a preheated grill, if liked.

COD CRÉOLE

This interesting pepper and tomato sauce makes ordinary cod something special. Serve with boiled rice.

ONE		TWO
7 g/¼ oz	**butter**	15 g/½ oz
½	**small onion, peeled and finely chopped**	1
½	**small green pepper, cored, seeded and sliced**	1
2.5 ml/½ tsp	**flour**	5 ml/1 tsp
½ × 225 g/8 oz	**can tomatoes, drained**	1 × 225 g/8 oz
15 ml/1 tbsp	**tomato purée**	30 ml/2 tbsp
	dash of hot pepper sauce	
30 ml/2 tbsp	**dry white wine or fish stock**	60 ml/4 tbsp
	salt	
100 g/4 oz	**cod fillet, skinned and cut into bite-sized pieces**	225 g/8 oz
	chopped fresh parsley, to garnish	

ONE

1. Place the butter, onion and pepper in a bowl. Cover and microwave on HIGH for 2 minutes. Stir in the flour, blending well.

2. Add the tomatoes, tomato purée, hot pepper sauce, wine or stock and salt to taste, blending well. Microwave on HIGH for 2–2½ minutes, stirring once.

3. Add the cod, cover and microwave on HIGH for a further 2–3 minutes or until the fish is cooked. Garnish with chopped parsley and serve at once.

TWO

1. Place the butter, onion and pepper in a bowl. Cover and microwave on HIGH for 4 minutes. Stir in the flour, blending well.

2. Add the tomatoes, tomato purée, hot pepper sauce, wine or stock and salt to taste, blending well. Microwave on HIGH for 4 minutes, stirring once.

3. Add the cod, cover and microwave on HIGH for a further 3–5 minutes or until the fish is cooked. Garnish with chopped parsley and serve at once.

CREAMY SEAFOOD PASTA

Almost any kind of cooked seafood may be used in this recipe; the quantities below give a good variety of textures, colours and flavours.

ONE		TWO
50 g/2 oz	**multi-coloured dried pasta twists or shells**	100 g/4 oz
300 ml/½ pint	**boiling fish or chicken stock**	450 ml/¾ pint
25 g/1oz	**canned tuna, flaked**	50 g/2 oz
25 g/1 oz	**large peeled prawns**	50 g/2 oz
25 g/1 oz	**fresh, frozen or canned cooked mussels**	50 g/2 oz
15 g/½ oz	**fresh, frozen or canned crabmeat, flaked**	25 g/1 oz
	Sauce:	
7 g/¼ oz	**butter**	15 g/½ oz
25 ml/1 fl oz	**double cream**	50 ml/2 fl oz
25 g/1 oz	**cream cheese**	50 g/2 oz
25 g/1 oz	**mild herb-flavoured cream cheese**	50 g/2 oz
	pinch of finely chopped fresh mixed herbs	
	salt and freshly ground black pepper	

ONE

1. Place the pasta in a deep bowl with the boiling stock. Cover and microwave on HIGH for 12–14 minutes then allow to stand for 5–10 minutes until tender.

2. Meanwhile mix the tuna with the prawns, mussels and crabmeat, blending well.

3. To make the sauce, place the butter and cream in a bowl. Microwave on HIGH for ¼–½ minute.

4. Gradually beat in the cream cheeses, the herbs and salt and pepper to taste.

5. Reduce the power setting to MEDIUM and microwave for 1 minute until hot, stirring once.

6. To serve, drain the pasta and toss with the fish mixture. Cover and microwave on HIGH for ½–1 minute to reheat.

7. Pour the sauce over the pasta and toss gently to mix. Serve at once with a crisp green salad, if liked.

TWO

1. Place the pasta in a deep bowl with the boiling stock. Cover and microwave on HIGH for 12–14 minutes then allow to stand for 5–10 minutes until tender.

2. Meanwhile mix the tuna with the prawns, mussels and crabmeat, blending well.

3. To make the sauce, place the butter and cream in a bowl. Microwave on HIGH for ½–¾ minute.

4. Gradually beat in the cream cheeses, the herbs and salt and pepper to taste.

5. Reduce the power setting to MEDIUM and microwave for 2 minutes until hot, stirring once.

6. To serve, drain the pasta and toss with the fish mixture. Cover and microwave on HIGH for 1–1½ minutes to reheat.

7. Pour the sauce over the pasta and toss gently to mix. Serve at once with a crisp green salad, if liked.

See photograph on page 28

POACHED SALMON WITH CUCUMBER HERB SAUCE

Pink, moist and succulent, fresh salmon may seem extravagant when cooking for 4, but costs little more than meat for a single or double serving.

ONE		TWO
one 175 g/6 oz	**salmon steaks, about 2.5 cm/1 inch thick**	two 175 g/6 oz
7 g/¼ oz	**butter**	15 g/½ oz
30 ml/2 tbsp	**dry vermouth**	60 ml/4 tbsp
	freshly ground black pepper	
	Sauce:	
40 g/1½ oz	**cucumber, cut into thin strips**	75 g/3 oz
7 g/¼ oz	**butter**	15 g/½ oz
5 ml/1 tsp	**snipped chives**	10 ml/2 tsp
5 ml/1 tsp	**chopped fresh tarragon or dill**	10 ml/2 tsp
5 ml/1 tsp	**flour**	10 ml/2 tsp
5 ml/1 tsp	**lemon juice**	10 ml/2 tsp
5 ml/1 tsp	**cream cheese**	10 ml/2 tsp
10 ml/2 tsp	**double cream**	20 ml/4 tsp
	salt and freshly ground black pepper	
	lemon slices and fresh tarragon or dill, to garnish	

ONE

1. Place the salmon steak in a small greased shallow dish. Dot with the butter, pour over the vermouth and sprinkle with black pepper. Cover with cling film and microwave on HIGH for 1½ minutes or until the fish flakes easily when tested with a fork. Transfer the salmon to a warmed serving dish. Reserve the cooking juices for the sauce.

2. To make the sauce, place the cucumber and butter in a small bowl. Cover and microwave on HIGH for 1½ minutes, stirring once. Add the herbs, blending well. Cover and microwave on HIGH for ½ minute.

3. Add the flour, blending well. Gradually add the reserved cooking juices, lemon juice and the cream cheese, beating well to blend. Microwave on HIGH for 1 minute, stirring once until smooth and thickened. Stir in the cream and salt and pepper to taste.

4. Spoon the sauce over the salmon. Garnish with lemon slices and sprigs of tarragon or dill and serve at once.

TWO

1. Place the salmon steaks in a small greased shallow dish. Dot with the butter, pour over the vermouth and sprinkle with black pepper. Cover with cling film and microwave on HIGH for 2–2½ minutes or until the fish flakes easily when tested with a fork. Transfer the salmon to a warmed serving dish. Reserve the cooking juices for the sauce.

2. To make the sauce, place the cucumber and butter in a small bowl. Cover and microwave on HIGH for 2–2½ minutes, stirring once. Add the herbs, blending well. Cover and microwave on HIGH for 1 minute.

3. Add the flour, blending well. Gradually add the reserved cooking juices, lemon juice and the cream cheese, beating well to blend. Microwave on HIGH for 1½ minutes, stirring once until smooth and thickened. Stir in the cream with salt and pepper to taste.

4. Spoon the sauce over the salmon. Garnish with lemon slices and sprigs of tarragon or dill and serve at once.

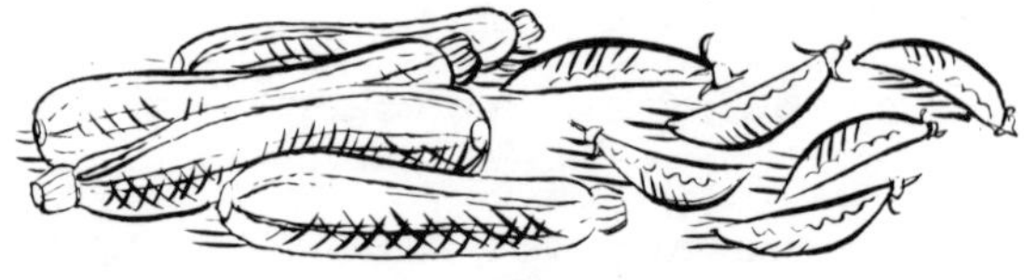

COOK'S TIP

Poached Salmon with Cucumber Herb Sauce is delicious served with Mangetout à la Française (see page 85) and Fantail Lemon Courgettes (see page 78).

See photograph on front jacket

Mackerel with gooseberry sauce (page 49) and Plaice with orange and walnut stuffing (page 50).

OVERLEAF

From left: Barbecued lamb with apricots (page 52); Stir fry lamb and courgettes (page 52) and Sweet and sour pork balls (page 54).

MACKEREL WITH GOOSEBERRY SAUCE

Tender, mouthwateringly rich mackerel needs a tart sauce like gooseberry to complement its flavour.

ONE		TWO
1	**mackerel, cleaned and gutted without heads**	2
4	**gooseberries, topped and tailed**	8
30 ml/2 tbsp	**water**	60 ml/4 tbsp
	salt and freshly ground black pepper	
1	**recipe hot Gooseberry Sauce (savoury version) (see page 101)**	1
	lemon slices and watercress sprigs, to garnish	

ONE

1. Using the tip of a sharp knife prick the gooseberries and use to stuff the mackerel. Place in a shallow dish and cut the skin in 2 or 3 places to prevent it from bursting. Pour over the water and season with salt and pepper to taste.

2. Cover and microwave on HIGH for 4–6 minutes until the fish flakes easily when tested with a fork.

3. Drain with a slotted spoon and transfer to a warmed serving plate. Spoon over the hot sauce, garnish with lemon slices and watercress sprigs.

TWO

1. Using the tip of a sharp knife prick the gooseberries and use to stuff the mackerel. Place in a shallow dish and cut the skin in 2 or 3 places to prevent it from bursting. Pour over the water and season with salt and pepper to taste.

2. Cover and microwave on HIGH for 8–10 minutes until the fish flakes easily when tested with a fork.

3. Drain with a slotted spoon and transfer to warmed serving plates. Spoon over the hot sauce, garnish with lemon slices and watercress sprigs.

Turkey breast parcels (page 70) with Poppy seed and pine nut potato salad (page 88).

KEDGEREE

This Victorian classic has recently become popular in fashionable restaurants countrywide. Serve as a supper dish or as part of a weekend brunch.

ONE		TWO
50 g/2 oz	**long-grain rice**	100 g/4 oz
300 ml/½ pint	**boiling water**	450 ml/¾ pint
	salt and freshly ground black pepper	
15 g/½ oz	**butter**	25 g/1 oz
2.5 ml/½ tsp	**finely grated lemon rind**	5 ml/1 tsp
100 g/4 oz	**cooked, smoked haddock, skinned, boned and flaked**	225 g/8 oz
7.5 ml/1½ tsp	**chopped fresh parsley**	15 ml/1 tbsp
	pinch of ground nutmeg	
10 ml/2 tsp	**double cream**	20 ml/4 tsp
½	**small hard-boiled egg, shelled and chopped**	1

ONE

1. Place the rice and water and salt to taste in a bowl. Cover and microwave on HIGH for 3 minutes. Reduce the power setting and microwave on MEDIUM for 12 minutes, stirring once. Leave to stand for 5 minutes then drain if necessary.

2. Place the butter and lemon rind in a bowl and microwave on HIGH for ½ minute to melt. Add the rice, haddock, parsley and salt, pepper and nutmeg to taste, blending well.

3. Fold in the cream and hard-boiled egg and microwave on HIGH for ½–¾ minute to reheat.

TWO

1. Place the rice and water and salt to taste in a bowl. Cover and microwave on HIGH for 3 minutes. Reduce the power setting and microwave on MEDIUM for 12 minutes, stirring once. Leave to stand for 5 minutes then drain if necessary.

2. Place the butter and lemon rind in a bowl and microwave on HIGH for 1 minute to melt. Add the rice, haddock, parsley and salt, pepper and nutmeg to taste, blending well.

3. Fold in the cream and hard-boiled egg and microwave on HIGH for ¾–1 minute to reheat.

PLAICE WITH ORANGE AND WALNUT STUFFING

Fish always gets my vote when it comes to microwave cooking because the flesh stays moist and succulent and cooking smells are minimal.

ONE		TWO
25 g/1 oz	**fresh white breadcrumbs**	50 g/2 oz
½	**finely grated rind and juice of a small orange**	1
2.5 ml/½ tsp	**chopped fresh parsley**	5 ml/1 tsp
7 g/¼ oz	**walnuts, chopped**	15 g/½ oz
	salt and freshly ground black pepper	
½	**egg, beaten**	1
2	**small plaice fillets, skinned**	4
7.5 ml/1½ tsp	**lemon juice**	15 ml/1 tbsp
7 g/¼ oz	**butter**	15 g/½ oz

ONE

1. Mix the breadcrumbs with the orange rind, parsley, walnuts, salt and pepper to taste and half of the orange juice, blending well. Bind together with the beaten egg.

2. Spread the stuffing over the plaice fillets and roll up from head to tail to make pinwheel shapes. Secure with wooden cocktail sticks.

3. Place in a cooking dish and spoon over the remaining orange juice and the lemon juice. Dot with the butter.

4. Cover and microwave on HIGH for 2 minutes or until the fish is opaque and flakes easily when tested with a fork. Stand for 5 minutes before serving.

TWO

1. Mix the breadcrumbs with the orange rind, parsley, walnuts, salt and pepper to taste and half of the orange juice, blending well. Bind together with the beaten egg.

2. Spread the stuffing over the plaice fillets and roll up from head to tail to make pinwheel shapes. Secure with wooden cocktail sticks.

3. Place in a cooking dish and spoon over the remaining orange juice and the lemon juice. Dot with the butter.

4. Cover and microwave on HIGH for 4 minutes or until the fish is opaque and flakes easily when tested with a fork. Stand for 5 minutes before serving.

See photograph on page 45

TUNA STUFFED PEPPERS

The secret in cooking these peppers so that they remain colourful yet tender is to par-cook them before stuffing.

ONE		TWO
1	**red, green or yellow peppers**	2
15 ml/1 tbsp	**water**	15 ml/1 tbsp
1	**small tomatoes, skinned, seeded and chopped**	2
½	**small onion, peeled and chopped**	1
15 ml/1 tbsp	**fresh white breadcrumbs**	30 ml/2 tbsp
50 g/2 oz	**canned tuna fish, drained and flaked**	100 g/4 oz
7.5 ml/1½ tsp	**tomato sauce or ketchup**	15 ml/1 tbsp
	salt and freshly ground black pepper	
	knob of butter	

ONE

1. Cut the top off the pepper and remove and discard the core and seeds. Place in a dish with the water. Cover and microwave on HIGH for 1½ minutes. Turn the pepper over and microwave on HIGH for a further 1½ minutes.

2. Meanwhile mix the tomato with the onion, breadcrumbs, tuna fish, tomato sauce and salt and pepper to taste, blending well. Spoon into the pepper.

3. Dot with a knob of butter. Cover and microwave on HIGH for 2 minutes. Leave to stand, covered, for 3 minutes before serving.

TWO

1. Cut the tops off the peppers and remove and discard the core and seeds. Place in a dish with the water. Cover and microwave on HIGH for 2½–3 minutes. Turn the peppers over and microwave on HIGH for a further 2½–3 minutes.

2. Meanwhile mix the tomato with the onion,

breadcrumbs, tuna fish, tomato sauce and salt and pepper to taste, blending well. Spoon into the peppers.

3. Dot with a knob of butter. Cover and microwave on HIGH for 4 minutes. Leave to stand, covered, for 3 minutes before serving.

COOK'S TIP

Try substituting canned salmon or crabmeat for tuna, or use cooked leftover chicken for a change.

TROUT WITH ALMONDS

Another classic dish made easy with the microwave. Serve with new potatoes and green beans to make a complete meal.

ONE		TWO
7.5 ml/1½ tsp	**lemon juice**	15 ml/1 tbsp
25 g/1 oz	**flaked almonds**	50 g/2 oz
15 g/½ oz	**butter**	25 g/1 oz
1	**medium trout, cleaned and gutted**	2
	lemon slices and parsley sprigs, to garnish	

ONE

1. Place the lemon juice, almonds and butter in a shallow dish. Microwave on HIGH for 1 minute to melt the butter.

2. Add the trout and turn on all sides to coat evenly with the buttered almond mixture. Cover and microwave on HIGH for 2–3 minutes, turning over once.

3. Allow to stand for 3 minutes or until the fish flakes easily when tested with a fork. Garnish with lemon slices and parsley sprigs and serve at once.

TWO

1. Place the lemon juice, almonds and butter in a shallow dish. Microwave on HIGH for 2 minutes to melt the butter.

2. Add the trout and turn on all sides to coat evenly with the buttered almond mixture. Cover and microwave on HIGH for 5 minutes, turning over once.

3. Allow to stand for 3 minutes or until the fish flakes easily when tested with a fork. Garnish with lemon slices and parsley sprigs and serve at once.

◆ ▪▪▪▪▪▪ ◆

'CODSWALLOP'

A tasty fish dish whose reputation after sampling surpasses its unfortunate name!

ONE		TWO
one 175 g/6 oz	**white fish fillets**	two 175 g/6 oz
½	**small onion, peeled and sliced**	1
1	**tomatoes, thinly sliced**	2
50 g/2 oz	**sweetcorn kernels**	100 g/4 oz
30 ml/2 tbsp	**dry cider**	60 ml/4 tbsp
	pinch of dried mixed herbs	
	salt and freshly ground black pepper	
15 ml/1 tbsp	**brown breadcrumbs**	30 ml/2 tbsp
15 g/½ oz	**Cheddar cheese, grated**	25 g/1 oz

ONE

1. Place the fish in a small gratin dish and cover with the onion, tomatoes and corn.

2. Pour over the cider and sprinkle with the herbs and salt and pepper to taste. Cover and microwave on HIGH for 3–4 minutes. Reduce the power setting to MEDIUM and cook for 3 minutes. Leave to stand for 5 minutes or until tender.

3. Sprinkle with the breadcrumbs and cheese. Brown under a preheated grill and serve at once.

TWO

1. Place the fish in a small gratin dish and cover with the onion, tomatoes and corn.

2. Pour over the cider and sprinkle with the herbs and salt and pepper to taste. Cover and microwave on HIGH for 6 minutes. Reduce the power setting to MEDIUM and cook for 5 minutes. Leave to stand for 5 minutes or until tender.

3. Sprinkle with the breadcrumbs and cheese. Brown under a preheated grill and serve at once.

STIR FRY LAMB AND COURGETTES

A light dish to make in Spring when English lamb and courgettes are at their best; and at only 160 calories per portion it makes a good meal to include in a calorie-controlled diet.

ONE		TWO
10 ml/2 tsp	**oil**	15 ml/1 tbsp
100 g/4 oz	**lamb leg steaks, cut into thin strips**	225 g/8 oz
100 g/4 oz	**courgettes, thinly sliced**	225 g/8 oz
4	**spring onions, trimmed and sliced**	8
½	**garlic clove, peeled and crushed**	1
15 ml/1 tbsp	**dry sherry**	30 ml/2 tbsp
	salt and freshly ground black pepper	

ONE

1. Preheat a browning dish on HIGH for 8 minutes or according to the manufacturer's instructions. Add the oil and microwave on HIGH for 1 minute.

2. Add the lamb and turn in the hot oil to brown evenly on all sides. Microwave on HIGH for 1½ minutes, stirring once.

3. Add the courgettes, spring onions and garlic, blending well, and microwave on HIGH for 2 minutes, stirring once.

4. Add the sherry and salt and pepper to taste, blending well. Microwave on HIGH for a further 1 minute. Serve at once with rice or noodles.

TWO

1. Preheat a browning dish on HIGH for 8 minutes or according to the manufacturer's instructions. Add the oil and microwave on HIGH for 1 minute.

2. Add the lamb and turn in the hot oil to brown evenly on all sides. Microwave on HIGH for 3 minutes, stirring once.

3. Add the courgettes, spring onions and garlic, blending well, and microwave on HIGH for 3–3½ minutes, stirring once.

4. Add the sherry and salt and pepper to taste, blending well. Microwave on HIGH for a further 1½–2 minutes. Serve at once with rice or noodles.

See photograph on page 46·47

BARBECUED LAMB WITH APRICOTS

Plain lamb cutlets are made special and given extra flavour in this recipe by cooking with dried apricots, onion, ginger, cucumber and spicy barbecue beans.

ONE		TWO
7.5 ml/1½ tsp	**oil**	15 ml/1 tbsp
½	**small onion, peeled and thinly sliced**	1
2	**small lamb cutlets, trimmed**	4
	pinch of ground ginger	
100 g/4 oz	**canned barbecue beans**	225 g/8 oz
25 g/1 oz	**dried apricots, soaked overnight in cold water**	50 g/2 oz
⅛	**cucumber, seeded and cut into thin strips**	¼
	salt and freshly ground black pepper	

ONE

1. Preheat a browning dish on HIGH for 8 minutes or according to the manufacturer's instructions.

2. Add the oil and microwave on HIGH for a further 1 minute.

3. Add the onion, lamb cutlets and ginger and turn in the hot oil to brown evenly on all sides. Microwave on HIGH for 2–3 minutes, turning over once.

4. Add the beans, the drained apricots, cucumber and salt and pepper to taste, blending well. Microwave on HIGH for 1½–2 minutes until hot and bubbling.

5. Serve at once with jacket baked potatoes.

TWO

1. Preheat a browning dish on HIGH for 8 minutes

or according to the manufacturer's instructions.

2. Add the oil and microwave on HIGH for a further 1 minute.

3. Add the onion, lamb cutlets and ginger and turn in the hot oil to brown evenly on all sides. Microwave on HIGH for 3–3½ minutes, turning over once.

4. Add the beans, the drained apricots, cucumber and salt and pepper to taste, blending well. Microwave on HIGH for 2½–3 minutes until hot and bubbling.

5. Serve at once with jacket baked potatoes.

See photograph on page 46·47

MUSTARD PORK STROGANOFF

Stroganoff is a dish that originates from Russia and is traditionally made with beef. The distinctive flavour of this dish results from the combination of paprika and soured cream. Here is a quick version using pork fillet.

ONE		TWO
225 g/8 oz	**pork fillet**	450 g/1 lb
15 g/½ oz	**butter**	25 g/1 oz
½	**small onion, peeled and chopped**	1
7.5 ml/1½ tsp	**sweet paprika**	15 ml/1 tbsp
2.5 ml/½ tsp	**mustard powder**	5 ml/1 tsp
45 ml/3 tbsp	**hot chicken stock**	75 ml/5 tbsp
7.5 ml/1½ tsp	**tomato purée**	15 ml/1 tbsp
45 ml/3 tbsp	**soured cream**	75 ml/5 tbsp
	salt and freshly ground black pepper	

ONE

1. Slice the pork into thin strips or medallions. Preheat a browning dish on HIGH for 8 minutes or according to the manufacturer's instructions.

2. Add the butter and swirl quickly to melt. Add the pork and turn quickly in the hot butter to brown evenly on all sides.

3. Add the onion and microwave on HIGH for 3 minutes, stirring once.

4. Add the paprika, mustard, stock and tomato purée, blending well. Cover and microwave on HIGH for 1–1½ minutes.

5. Stir in the soured cream and salt and pepper to taste. Serve hot with buttered tagliatelle.

TWO

1. Slice the pork into thin strips or medallions. Preheat a browning dish on HIGH for 8 minutes or according to the manufacturer's instructions.

2. Add the butter and swirl quickly to melt. Add the pork and turn quickly in the hot butter to brown evenly on all sides.

3. Add the onion and microwave on HIGH for 5 minutes, stirring once.

4. Add the paprika, mustard, stock and tomato purée, blending well. Cover and microwave on HIGH for 2½ minutes.

5. Stir in the soured cream and salt and pepper to taste. Serve hot with buttered tagliatelle.

SWEET AND SOUR PORK BALLS

Red, yellow and green peppers add colour and charm to this simple dish. Serve with boiled rice, ribbon noodles or a crisp seasonal salad.

ONE		TWO
175 g/6 oz	**minced raw pork**	350 g/12 oz
½	**small onion, peeled and chopped**	1
	salt and freshly ground black pepper	
10 ml/2 tsp	**oil**	15 ml/1 tbsp
¼	**red pepper, cored, seeded and sliced**	½
¼	**yellow pepper, cored, seeded and sliced**	½
¼	**green pepper, cored, seeded and sliced**	½
7.5 ml/1½ tsp	**red wine vinegar**	15 ml/1 tbsp
7.5 ml/1½ tsp	**demerara sugar**	15 ml/1 tbsp
2.5 ml/½ tsp	**soy sauce**	5 ml/1 tsp
37.5 ml/2½ tbsp	**unsweetened orange juice**	75 ml/5 tbsp
37.5 ml/2½ tbsp	**chicken stock**	75 ml/5 tbsp
	pinch of ground ginger	
	pinch of Chinese 5 spice powder	
5ml/1 tsp	**cornflour**	10 ml/2 tsp

ONE

1. Mix the pork with the onion and salt and pepper to taste, blending well. Divide the mixture into 4 and shape into meatballs.

2. Preheat a browning dish on HIGH for 8 minutes or according to the manufacturer's instructions.

3. Add the oil to the browning dish and swirl to coat the base of the dish. Microwave on HIGH for a further 1 minute.

4. Add the meatballs and turn in the hot oil to brown evenly. Microwave on HIGH for 2½–3 minutes, turning over once.

5. Remove the meatballs with a slotted spoon and set aside. Add the peppers to the juices in the dish, blending well. Cover and microwave on HIGH for 2½–3 minutes, stirring once.

6. Add the vinegar, sugar, soy sauce, orange juice, stock, ginger, Chinese 5 spice powder and salt and pepper to taste, blending well. Microwave on HIGH for 1–1½ minutes.

7. Mix the cornflour to a smooth paste with a little water. Stir into the pepper mixture, blending well. Microwave on HIGH for ½–¾ minute, stirring twice.

8. Return the meatballs to the dish and baste with the sauce. Microwave on HIGH for 1–1½ minutes. Serve at once.

TWO

1. Mix the pork with the onion and salt and pepper to taste, blending well. Divide the mixture into 8 and shape into meatballs.

2. Preheat a browning dish on HIGH for 8 minutes or according to the manufacturer's instructions.

3. Add the oil to the browning dish and swirl to coat the base of the dish. Microwave on HIGH for a further 1 minute.

4. Add the meatballs and turn in the hot oil to brown evenly. Microwave on HIGH for 4 minutes, turning over once.

5. Remove the meatballs with a slotted spoon and set aside. Add the peppers to the juices in the dish, blending well. Cover and microwave on HIGH for 4 minutes, stirring once.

6. Add the vinegar, sugar, soy sauce, orange juice, stock, ginger, Chinese 5 spice powder and salt and pepper to taste, blending well. Microwave on HIGH for 2 minutes.

7. Mix the cornflour to a smooth paste with a little water. Stir into the pepper mixture, blending well. Microwave on HIGH for 1 minute, stirring twice.

8. Return the meatballs to the dish and baste with the sauce. Microwave on HIGH for 2 minutes. Serve at once.

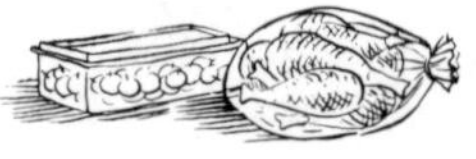

FREEZABILITY

Sweet and Sour Pork Balls will freeze well for up to 3 months.

See photograph on page 46·47

CHINESE PORK AND PASTA

Pasta twists or spirals make this stir-fried pork and vegetable concoction a good hearty dish to satisfy after work appetites.

ONE		TWO
20 ml/4 tsp	**soy sauce**	45 ml/3 tbsp
10 ml/2 tsp	**sherry**	20 ml/4 tsp
10 ml/2 tsp	**cornflour**	20 ml/4 tsp
	salt and freshly ground black pepper	
100 g/4 oz	**pork fillet, cubed**	225 g/8 oz
50 g/2 oz	**dried pasta twists or spirals**	100 g/4 oz
300 ml/½ pint	**boiling water**	450 ml/¾ pint
7.5 ml/1½ tsp	**oil**	15 ml/1 tbsp
¼	**green pepper, cored, seeded and sliced**	½
¼	**red pepper, cored, seeded and sliced**	½
2	**spring onions, chopped**	4
40 g/1½ oz	**beansprouts**	75 g/3 oz

ONE

1. Mix the soy sauce with the sherry, cornflour and salt and pepper to taste, blending well. Add the pork fillet and leave to marinate for 30 minutes.

2. Place the pasta in a deep bowl with the boiling water. Cover and microwave on HIGH for 12–14 minutes then allow to stand for 5–10 minutes until tender. Drain and refresh under cold running water.

3. Preheat a browning dish on HIGH for 8 minutes or according to the manufacturer's instructions.

4. Add the oil to the browning dish and swirl to coat the base of the dish. Microwave on HIGH for a further 1 minute.

5. Remove the pork from the marinade with a slotted spoon and add to the browning dish. Turn quickly in the hot oil to brown evenly on all sides. Add the peppers and microwave on HIGH for 2 minutes, stirring once.

6. Add the spring onions and beansprouts, blending well. Microwave on HIGH for 3 minutes, stirring once.

7. Stir in the cooked pasta and marinade, blending well. Microwave on HIGH for 1 minute, stirring twice until the sauce is boiling and thickened. Serve at once.

TWO

1. Mix the soy sauce with the sherry, cornflour and salt and pepper to taste, blending well. Add the pork fillet and leave to marinate for 30 minutes.

2. Place the pasta in a deep bowl with the boiling water. Cover and microwave on HIGH for 12–14 minutes then allow to stand for 5–10 minutes. Drain and refresh under cold running water.

3. Preheat a browning dish on HIGH for 8 minutes or according to the manufacturer's instructions.

4. Add the oil to the browning dish and swirl to coat the base of the dish. Microwave on HIGH for a further 1 minute.

5. Remove the pork from the marinade with a slotted spoon and add to the browning dish. Turn quickly in the hot oil to brown evenly on all sides. Add the peppers and microwave on HIGH for 3½ minutes, stirring once.

6. Add the spring onions and beansprouts, blending well. Microwave on HIGH for 4½–5 minutes, stirring once.

7. Stir in the cooked pasta and marinade, blending well. Microwave on HIGH for 1½–2 minutes, stirring twice until the sauce is boiling and thickened. Serve at once.

HONEY GLAZED PORK CHOPS

This quick and easy recipe brings new life to ordinary, mid-week pork chops. The combination of cider and honey makes the meat tender and juicy while adding a delicious flavour.

ONE		TWO
1	**large pork loin chops**	2
	salt and freshly ground black pepper	
7.5 ml/1½ tsp	**clear honey**	15 ml/1 tbsp
45 ml/3 tbsp	**dry cider**	75 ml/5 tbsp
2.5 ml/½ tsp	**dried sage**	5 ml/1 tsp

ONE

1. Preheat a browning dish on HIGH for 8 minutes or according to the manufacturer's instructions.

2. Season the pork with salt and pepper to taste. Add to the browning dish then turn over quickly to brown evenly on both sides. Transfer to a shallow dish.

3. Mix the honey with the cider and sage. Pour over the chop and microwave on HIGH for 5–7 minutes, turning over and basting once. Leave to stand, covered for 3 minutes.

4. Serve the pork chop with the sauce poured over.

TWO

1. Preheat a browning dish on HIGH for 8 minutes or according to the manufacturer's instructions.

2. Season the pork with salt and pepper to taste. Add to the browning dish then turn over quickly to brown evenly on both sides. Transfer to a shallow dish.

3. Mix the honey with the cider and sage. Pour over the chops and microwave on HIGH for 12–14 minutes, turning over and basting once. Leave to stand, covered, for 3 minutes.

4. Serve the pork chops with the sauce poured over.

DANISH VÉRONIQUE

Danish Véronique is the ideal dish when entertaining – succulent pink gammon steaks cooked in a creamy sauce with black grapes. Serve with a selection of perfectly cooked vegetables.

ONE		TWO
1 × 175 g/6 oz	**gammon steaks**	2 × 175 g/6 oz
30 ml/2 tbsp	**dry white wine**	60 ml/4 tbsp
¼	**small onion, finely chopped**	½
15 g/½ oz	**butter**	25 g/1 oz
15 g/½ oz	**flour**	25 g/1 oz
75 ml/5 tbsp	**milk**	150 ml/¼ pint
15 ml/1 tbsp	**single cream**	30 ml/2 tbsp
	freshly ground black pepper	
50 g/2 oz	**black grapes, halved and seeded**	100 g/4 oz
	fresh dill sprigs, to garnish	

ONE

1. Remove the rind from the gammon and snip the fat with kitchen scissors at regular intervals to prevent it curling during cooking. Place in a shallow dish with the wine and onion. Cover and microwave on MEDIUM for 8 minutes until cooked.

2. Place the butter in a bowl and microwave on HIGH for ½ minute to melt. Add the flour, blending well. Gradually add the milk and the strained juices from the gammon. Microwave on HIGH for 1–2 minutes, stirring three times until smooth.

3. Stir in the cream and pepper to taste. Add half of the grapes and microwave on HIGH for ½ minute to reheat.

4. To serve, pour the sauce over the gammon, garnish with the remaining grapes and the fresh dill sprigs.

TWO

1. Remove the rind from the gammon and snip the fat with kitchen scissors at regular intervals to prevent it curling during cooking. Place in a shallow dish with the wine and onion. Cover and microwave on MEDIUM for 13–15 minutes until cooked.

2. Place the butter in a bowl and microwave on HIGH for ¾ minute to melt. Add the flour, blending well. Gradually add the milk and the strained juices from the gammon. Microwave on HIGH for 3½ minutes, stirring three times until smooth.

3. Stir in the cream and pepper to taste. Add half of the grapes and microwave on HIGH for 1 minute to reheat.

4. To serve, pour the sauce over the gammon, garnish with the remaining grapes and the fresh dill sprigs.

BRAISED GAMMON STEAKS WITH CHICORY AND MUSHROOM SAUCE

This tasty combination of gammon steaks, tender chicory and a rich creamy mushroom sauce will prove a winner for both mid-week and special occasion entertaining. Serve with boiled new potatoes and a crisp salad.

ONE		TWO
1 × 100 g/4 oz	**middle cut gammon steaks, rind removed**	2 × 100 g/4 oz
	few sprigs fresh rosemary	
60 ml/4 tbsp	**cider**	90 ml/6 tbsp
1	**heads chicory, trimmed and halved**	2
7 g/¼ oz	**butter**	15 g/½ oz
7.5 ml/1½ tsp	**cornflour**	15 ml/1 tbsp
25 g/1 oz	**mushrooms, wiped and chopped**	50 g/2 oz
7.5 ml/1½ tsp	**double cream**	15 ml/1 tbsp
	salt and freshly ground black pepper	

ONE

1. Using kitchen scissors snip the gammon rind at regular intervals to prevent it from curling during cooking. Place in a shallow dish, sprinkle with a little rosemary and pour over the cider. Cover and leave to marinate for 2 hours.

2. Add the chicory to the gammon, cover and microwave on HIGH for 2½–3½ minutes until tender.

3. Meanwhile, blend the butter with the cornflour in a bowl. Strain the juices from the gammon and chicory and gradually add to the cornflour mixture, blending well. Stir in the mushrooms and microwave on HIGH for 2–2½ minutes until smooth and thickened, stirring twice.

4. Allow to cool slightly then stir in the cream and salt and pepper to taste. Spoon the sauce over the gammon and microwave on HIGH for ½ minute to reheat. Serve at once.

TWO

1. Using kitchen scissors snip the gammon rind at regular intervals to prevent it from curling during cooking. Place in a shallow dish, sprinkle with a little rosemary and pour over the cider. Cover and leave to marinate for 2 hours.

2. Add the chicory to the gammon, cover and microwave on HIGH for 5–7 minutes until tender.

3. Meanwhile, blend the butter with the cornflour in a bowl. Strain the juices from the gammon and chicory and gradually add to the cornflour mixture, blending well. Stir in the mushrooms and microwave on HIGH for 3–4 minutes until smooth and thickened, stirring twice.

4. Allow to cool slightly then stir in the cream with salt and pepper to taste. Spoon the sauce over the gammon and microwave on HIGH for ¾–1 minute to reheat. Serve at once.

TAGLIATELLE WITH HAM AND PEAS

There is little time saving when cooking pasta in the microwave but the bonus is that there are no sticky pans and steamy kitchens to contend with. This is a very attractive pasta dish with its contrasting green and pink and it is literally made in minutes.

ONE		TWO
100 g/4 oz	**dried tagliatelle verdi**	225 g/8 oz
300 ml/½ pint	**boiling water**	600 ml/1 pint
	salt and freshly ground black pepper	
25 g/1 oz	**cooked ham, cut into thin strips**	50 g/2 oz
25 g/1 oz	**frozen peas**	50 g/2 oz
75 ml/5 tbsp	**single cream**	150 ml/¼ pint

ONE

1. Place the pasta in a deep bowl with the boiling water and salt to taste. Cover and microwave on HIGH for 6 minutes then allow to stand for 3 minutes until tender.

2. Drain the pasta, return to the bowl and add the ham, peas, cream and salt and pepper to taste, blending well. Microwave on HIGH for 2 minutes.

3. Toss gently to mix and serve at once.

TWO

1. Place the pasta in a deep bowl with the boiling water and salt to taste. Cover and microwave on HIGH for 6 minutes then allow to stand for 3 minutes until tender.

2. Drain the pasta, return to the bowl and add the ham, peas, cream and salt and pepper to taste, blending well. Microwave on HIGH for 2 minutes.

3. Toss gently to mix and serve at once.

STORECUPBOARD STANDBY

This tasty dish is easily made on the spur of the moment from a well-stocked storecupboard and refrigerator.

GINGERED BACON WITH PINEAPPLE

Pineapple makes a tasty addition to any gammon or bacon dish – here it is combined with ginger and lemon juice to make a spicy sauce for bacon chops.

ONE		TWO
2 × 75 g/3 oz	**bacon chops**	4 × 75 g/3 oz
½ × 225 g/8 oz	**can pineapple slices in natural juice**	1 × 225 g/8 oz
30 ml/2 tbsp	**dry white wine or vermouth**	60 ml/4 tbsp
7.5 ml/1½ tsp	**lemon juice**	15 ml/1 tbsp
7.5 ml/1½ tsp	**dark brown sugar**	15 ml/1 tbsp
5 ml/1 tsp	**ground ginger**	10 ml/2 tsp
5 ml/1 tsp	**Worcestershire sauce**	10 ml/2 tsp
	dash of Tabasco sauce	
1.25 ml/¼ tsp	**Dijon mustard**	2.5 ml/½ tsp
5 ml/1 tsp	**cornflour**	10 ml/2 tsp
	watercress sprigs, to garnish	

ONE

1. Using kitchen scissors, snip the bacon fat at regular intervals to prevent it from curling during cooking. Place in a shallow dish.

2. Drain the juice from the pineapple and mix with the wine or vermouth, lemon juice, sugar, ginger, Worcestershire sauce, Tabasco, mustard and cornflour, blending well.

3. Pour over the chops, cover and microwave on HIGH for 3½–4 minutes until tender, turning over once.

4. Arrange the pineapple slices on top of the chop,

cover and microwave on HIGH for ¾ minute. Leave to stand, covered, for 5 minutes. Garnish with watercress sprigs and serve at once.

TWO

1. Using kitchen scissors, snip the bacon fat at regular intervals to prevent it from curling during cooking. Place in a shallow dish.

2. Drain the juice from the pineapple and mix with the wine or vermouth, lemon juice, sugar, ginger, Worcestershire sauce, Tabasco, mustard and cornflour, blending well.

3. Pour over the chops, cover and microwave on HIGH for 5 minutes until tender, turning over once.

4. Arrange the pineapple slices on top of the chops, cover and microwave on HIGH for 1 minute. Leave to stand, covered, for 5 minutes. Garnish with watercress sprigs and serve at once.

COOK'S TIP

For a stronger flavour, and if time permits, marinate the bacon chops in the sauce for up to 8 hours before cooking.

PASTA WITH BACON, TOMATOES AND PEPPER

It is not easy to conjure up economical, yet interesting and tasty dishes every day; this dish fits the bill perfectly by 'stretching' bacon, tomatoes and peppers with economical short-cut pasta.

ONE		TWO
100 g/4 oz	**dried pasta twists or spirals**	225 g/8 oz
450 ml/¾ pint	**boiling water**	900 ml/1½ pints
2	**rashers streaky bacon, rinded**	4
½ × 225 g/8 oz	**can tomatoes, drained and coarsely chopped**	1 × 225 g/8 oz
½	**small garlic cloves, peeled and crushed**	1
½	**small red pepper, cored, seeded and chopped**	1
	salt and freshly ground black pepper	
	chopped fresh parsley, to garnish	

ONE

1. Place the pasta in a deep bowl with the boiling water. Cover and microwave on HIGH for 12–14 minutes then allow to stand for 5–10 minutes until tender.

2. Meanwhile place the bacon on a plate and cover with a sheet of absorbent kitchen towel. Microwave on HIGH for 1½–2 minutes or until cooked and crisp. Cut into bite-sized pieces.

3. Place the tomatoes, garlic, red pepper and salt and pepper to taste in a bowl. Cover and microwave on HIGH for 2–3 minutes, stirring once. Add the bacon, blending well.

4. Drain the pasta and mix with the sauce, tossing well to coat.

5. Garnish with parsley and serve at once.

TWO

1. Place the pasta in a deep bowl with the boiling water. Cover and microwave on HIGH for 12–14 minutes then allow to stand for 5–10 minutes.

2. Meanwhile place the bacon on a plate and cover with a sheet of absorbent kitchen towel. Microwave on HIGH for 3–3½ minutes or until cooked and crisp. Cut into bite-sized pieces.

3. Place the tomatoes, garlic, pepper and salt and pepper to taste in a bowl. Cover and microwave on HIGH for 4–5 minutes, stirring once. Add the bacon, blending well.

4. Drain the pasta and mix with the sauce, tossing well to coat.

5. Garnish with parsley and serve at once.

STORECUPBOARD STANDBY

This dish is a good standby using ingredients from a well-stocked cupboard and refrigerator. If you have leftover cooked pasta just microwave on HIGH for 2 minutes to reheat before mixing with the sauce. Try using cooked rice instead of pasta for a change.

SIZZLING FILLET WITH YOGURT SAUCE

A sizzling fillet steak is a treat at any time but it takes on kingly proportions when served with this piquant yogurt sauce. A simple mixed salad or crisp green vegetable is the only accompaniment that it needs.

ONE		TWO
1 × 225 g/8 oz	**piece fillet steak**	1 × 450 g/1 lb
	salt and freshly ground black pepper	
15 g/½ oz	**butter**	25 g/1 oz
30 ml/2 tbsp	**natural yogurt**	60 ml/4 tbsp
1.25 ml/¼ tsp	**sugar**	2.5 ml/½ tsp
5 ml/1 tsp	**green peppercorns**	10 ml/2 tsp

ONE

1. Preheat a browning dish on HIGH for 8 minutes or according to the manufacturer's instructions.

2. Season the steak on all sides with salt and pepper to taste.

3. Add the butter to the browning dish and microwave on HIGH for ½ minute. Add the steak and turn quickly in the hot oil to brown evenly on all sides. Microwave on HIGH for 2–3 minutes, turning over once.

4. Remove from the dish, carve into thick slices and arrange on a warmed serving dish.

5. Add the yogurt, sugar and peppercorns to the juices in the dish, blending well. Microwave on HIGH for ½ minute, stirring once. Spoon over the steak and serve at once.

TWO

1. Preheat a browning dish on HIGH for 8 minutes or according to the manufacturer's instructions.

2. Season the steak on all sides with salt and pepper.

3. Add the butter to the browning dish and microwave on HIGH for ½ minute. Add the steak and turn quickly in the hot oil to brown evenly on all sides. Microwave on HIGH for 5–6 minutes, turning over once.

4. Remove from the dish, carve into thick slices and arrange on a warmed serving dish.

5. Add the yogurt, sugar and peppercorns to the juices in the dish, blending well. Microwave on HIGH for ¾–1 minute, stirring once. Spoon over the steak and serve at once.

STEAK AU POIVRE

This is one of the simplest, quickest and most sophisticated main meals I know. Contrary to popular belief the microwave will cook the steak deliciously pink and rare on the inside while mouthwateringly seared and brown on the outside.

ONE		TWO
1 × 225 g/8 oz	**piece fillet steak**	1 × 450 g/1 lb
7.5 ml/1½ tsp	**crushed black peppercorns**	15 ml/1 tbsp
	salt	
15 g/½ oz	**butter**	25 g/1 oz
10 ml/2 tsp	**brandy or Madeira**	15 ml/1 tbsp
30 ml/2 tbsp	**double cream**	60 ml/4 tbsp

ONE

1. Preheat a browning dish on HIGH for 8 minutes or according to the manufacturer's instructions.

2. Roll the steak in the crushed peppercorns to coat all sides. Season to taste with a little salt.

3. Add the butter to the browning dish and microwave on HIGH for ½ minute. Add the steak and turn quickly in the hot butter to brown evenly on all sides. Microwave on HIGH for 2–3 minutes, turning over once.

4. Remove from the dish, carve into thick slices and arrange on a warmed serving dish.

5. Add the brandy or Madeira to the juices in the browning dish, blending well. Microwave on HIGH for ½–¾ minute, stirring once. Spoon over the steak and serve at once.

TWO

1. Preheat a browning dish on HIGH for 8 minutes or according to the manufacturer's instructions.

2. Roll the steak in the crushed peppercorns to coat on all sides. Season to taste with a little salt.

3. Add the butter to the browning dish and microwave on HIGH for ½ minute. Add the steak and turn quickly in the hot butter to brown evenly on all sides. Microwave on HIGH for 5–6 minutes, turning over once.

4. Remove from the dish, carve into thick slices and arrange on a warmed serving dish.

5. Add the brandy or Madeira to the juices in the browning dish, blending well. Microwave on HIGH for 1 minute, stirring once. Spoon over the steak and serve at once.

BEEF STROGANOFF

It is essential to follow the timings in this recipe exactly for mouth-wateringly tender strips of beef. Serve with boiled rice and a green salad to make a quick and delicious meal.

ONE		TWO
7 g/¼ oz	**butter**	15 g/½ oz
175 g/6 oz	**beef fillet, cut into thin strips**	350 g/12 oz
½	**small onion, peeled and chopped**	1
50 g/2 oz	**button mushrooms, wiped and finely sliced**	100 g/4 oz
7 g/¼ oz	**plain flour**	15 g/½ oz
25 ml/1 fl oz	**dry white wine**	50 ml/2 fl oz
	salt and freshly ground black pepper	
45 ml/3 tbsp	**soured cream**	75 ml/5 tbsp
	chopped fresh parsley, to garnish	

ONE

1. Preheat a browning dish on HIGH for 8 minutes or according to the manufacturer's instructions. Add the butter and microwave on HIGH for ½ minute to melt.

2. Add the beef and turn quickly in the hot butter to brown evenly on all sides. Microwave on HIGH for 1–2 minutes until just tender and pink.

3. Remove the meat from the dish with a slotted spoon and set aside. Add the onion and mushrooms to the juices in the dish and microwave on HIGH for 2 minutes, stirring once.

4. Stir in the flour, blending well. Gradually add the wine, then the beef and salt and pepper to taste. Microwave on HIGH for ¾–1 minute, stirring twice. Stir in the soured cream, blending well. Serve at once garnished with chopped parsley.

TWO

1. Preheat a browning dish on HIGH for 8 minutes or according to the manufacturer's instructions. Add the butter and microwave on HIGH for ½ minute to melt.

2. Add the beef and turn quickly in the hot butter to brown evenly on all sides. Microwave on HIGH for 2–3 minutes until just tender and pink.

3. Remove the meat from the dish with a slotted spoon and set aside. Add the onion and mushrooms to the juices in the dish and microwave on HIGH for 3–3½ minutes, stirring one.

4. Stir in the flour, blending well. Gradually add the wine, beef and salt and pepper to taste. Microwave on HIGH for 1½–2 minutes, stirring twice. Stir in the soured cream, blending well. Serve at once garnished with chopped parsley.

STEAK AND KIDNEY SUET PUDDING

Suet puddings with their traditionally long steaming times are seldom the ideal choice when cooking for 1 or 2. However, the microwave brings them to the fore again with its speed of cooking. This is a really hearty dish, so serve with just an accompaniment of vegetables in season.

ONE		TWO
100 g/4 oz	**minced steak**	225 g/8 oz
1	**lamb's kidneys, skinned, cored and sliced**	2
10 ml/2 tsp	**flour**	15 ml/1 tbsp
	salt and freshly ground black pepper	
7 g/ ¼ oz	**butter**	15 g/½ oz
½	**small onion, peeled and chopped**	1
75 ml/5 tbsp	**boiling beef stock**	150 ml/¼ pint
	pinch of dried mixed herbs	
25 g/1 oz	**mushrooms, wiped and sliced**	50 g/2 oz
	Suet Pastry:	
50 g/2 oz	**self-raising flour**	100 g/4 oz
	pinch of salt	
1.25 ml/¼ tsp	**baking powder**	2.5 ml/½ tsp
25 g/1 oz	**shredded beef suet**	50 g/2 oz
37.5 ml/2½ tbsp	**water**	75 ml/5 tbsp

ONE

1. Place the minced steak and the kidney in a bowl. Add the flour and salt and pepper to taste and toss together.

2. Place the butter in a bowl and microwave on HIGH for ½ minute to melt.

3. Add the steak and kidney mixture and the onion. Cover and microwave on HIGH for ¾ minute. Break up with a fork and microwave on HIGH for a further ¾ minute.

4. Add the stock and herbs, blending well. Cover and microwave on HIGH for 2 minutes. Stir well to blend, reduce the power setting to MEDIUM and microwave for a further 6 minutes, stirring once.

5. Meanwhile, make the pastry. Sift the flour, salt and baking powder together and stir in the suet, blending well. Bind together with the water to make a firm but pliable dough.

6. Roll out two-thirds of the pastry and use to line a lightly greased 300 ml/½ pint pudding basin.

7. Spoon the filling into the basin with the mushrooms. Roll out the remaining pastry to make a lid and place on top of the pudding, pressing the edges together to seal. Make a small hole in the lid to let the steam escape during cooking.

8. Cover loosely with absorbent kitchen towel and microwave on MEDIUM for 4–5 minutes. Allow to stand for 5 minutes before serving.

TWO

1. Place the minced steak and kidney in a bowl. Add the flour and salt and pepper to taste and toss together.

2. Place the butter in a bowl and microwave on HIGH for ½ minute to melt.

3. Add the steak and kidney mixture and onion. Cover and microwave on HIGH for 1 minute. Break up with a fork and microwave on HIGH for a further 1 minute.

4. Add the stock and herbs, blending well. Cover and microwave on HIGH for 3 minutes. Stir well to blend, reduce the power setting to MEDIUM and microwave for a further 7–8 minutes, stirring once.

5. Meanwhile make the pastry. Sift the flour, salt and baking powder together and stir in the suet, blending well. Bind together with the water to make a firm but pliable dough.

6. Roll out two-thirds of the pastry and use to line 2 lightly greased 300 ml/½ pint pudding basins.

7. Spoon the filling into the basins with the mushrooms. Roll out the remaining pastry to make lids and place in position. Make holes in the lids to help the steam to escape during cooking.

8. Cover loosely with absorbent kitchen towel and microwave on MEDIUM for 7–8 minutes. Allow to stand for 5 minutes before serving.

BEEF AND ORANGE RISOTTO

This colourful 'one pot' meal has a wholesome and hearty feel when made with brown rice. If you prefer to use white rice instead reduce the rice cooking time by 5 minutes.

ONE		TWO
5 ml/1 tsp	**oil**	10 ml/2 tsp
75 g/3 oz	**rump steak, cut into thin slivers**	175 g/6 oz
¼	**onion, peeled and chopped**	½
½	**garlic clove, peeled and crushed**	1
¼	**red pepper, cored, seeded and cut into strips**	½
25 g/1 oz	**button mushrooms, halved**	50 g/2 oz
50 g/2 oz	**brown rice**	100 g/4 oz
75 ml/5 tbsp	**beef stock**	150 ml/¼ pint
100 ml/4 fl oz	**unsweetened orange juice**	200 ml/8 fl oz
7.5 ml/1½ tsp	**Worcestershire sauce**	15 ml/1 tbsp
7.5 ml/1½ tsp	**tomato purée**	15 ml/1 tbsp
7.5 ml/1½ tsp	**chopped fresh parsley**	15 ml/1 tbsp
	salt and freshly ground black pepper	
	orange slices and parsley sprigs, to garnish	

ONE

1. Preheat a browning dish on HIGH for 8 minutes or according to the manufacturer's instructions.

2. Add the oil and steak and turn quickly on all sides to brown evenly.

3. Add the onion, garlic, red pepper, mushrooms and rice, blending well. Microwave on HIGH for 3–4 minutes, stirring once.

4. Transfer to a bowl and add the stock and orange juice, blending well. Cover and microwave on HIGH for 15 minutes.

5. Add the Worcestershire sauce, tomato purée, parsley and salt and pepper to taste, blending well. Cover and microwave on HIGH for 5–8 minutes until the rice is tender and all the liquid has been absorbed.

6. Serve at once garnished with orange slices and parsley sprigs.

TWO

1. Preheat a small browning dish on HIGH for 8 minutes or according to the manufacturer's instructions.

2. Add the oil and steak and turn quickly on all sides to brown evenly.

3. Add the onion, garlic, red pepper, mushrooms and rice, blending well. Microwave on HIGH for 3–4 minutes, stirring once.

4. Transfer to a bowl and add the stock and orange juice, blending well. Cover and microwave on HIGH for 15 minutes.

5. Add the Worcestershire sauce, tomato purée, parsley and salt and pepper to taste, blending well. Cover and microwave on HIGH for 5–8 minutes until the rice is tender and all the liquid has been absorbed.

6. Serve at once garnished with orange slices and parsley sprigs.

MUSHROOM STEAKLETS

A welcome change from plain hamburgers – mushroom steaklets are tasty burgers made with beef, mushrooms and sage.

ONE		TWO
7 g/¼ oz	**butter**	15 g/½ oz
½	**small onion, peeled and finely chopped**	1
50 g/2 oz	**mushrooms, wiped and finely chopped**	100 g/4 oz
175 g/6 oz	**lean minced beef**	350 g/12 oz
	pinch of dried sage	
	salt and freshly ground black pepper	
	a little beaten egg, to bind	

ONE

1. Place the butter, onion and mushrooms in a bowl. Microwave on HIGH for 1½–2½ minutes until tender, stirring once.

2. Add the beef, sage, salt and pepper to taste and sufficient beaten egg to bind. Mix thoroughly to blend then shape into a hamburger.

3. Preheat a greased browning dish on HIGH for 8 minutes or according to the manufacturer's instructions.

4. Add the mushroom steaklet and microwave on HIGH for 2½–3½ minutes, turning over twice. Serve hot in a hamburger bun with a crisp salad or vegetables.

TWO

1. Place the butter, onion and mushrooms in a bowl. Microwave on HIGH for 3–4 minutes until tender, stirring once.

2. Add the beef, sage, salt and pepper to taste and sufficient beaten egg to bind. Mix thoroughly to blend then shape into a hamburger.

3. Preheat a greased browning dish on HIGH for 8 minutes or according to the manufacturer's instructions.

4. Add the mushroom steaklet and microwave on HIGH for 6–7 minutes, turning over twice. Serve hot in a hamburger bun with a crisp salad or vegetables.

SIMPLEST SPAGHETTI BOLOGNESE

Perfectly cooked spaghetti and a delicious version of the famous Italian bolognese sauce feature in this easy main meal. Serve with freshly grated Parmesan cheese for sprinkling and a crisp side salad.

ONE		TWO
50 g/2 oz	**dried spaghetti**	100 g/4 oz
500 ml/14 fl oz	**boiling water**	1 litre/1¾ pints
	salt and freshly ground black pepper	
	Bolognese Sauce:	
100 g/4 oz	**minced beef**	225 g/8 oz
½	**small onion, peeled and finely chopped**	1
2.5 ml/½ tsp	**garlic purée**	5 ml/1 tsp
½	**small green pepper, cored, seeded and chopped**	1
7.5 ml/1½ tsp	**tomato purée**	15 ml/1 tbsp
½ × 225 g/8 oz	**can chopped tomatoes**	1 × 225 g/8 oz
2.5 ml/½ tsp	**Worcestershire sauce**	3 ml/¾ tsp
2.5 ml/½ tsp	**dried oregano**	5 ml/1 tsp

ONE

1. Break the spaghetti in half and place in a deep bowl with the water and salt to taste. Cover and microwave on HIGH for 10 minutes, stirring once. Leave to stand, covered, for 5 minutes until tender.

2. Place the beef, onion, garlic purée and pepper in a bowl. Microwave on HIGH for 2 minutes, stirring once.

3. Add the tomato purée, tomatoes, Worcestershire sauce, oregano and salt and pepper to taste, blending well. Cover and microwave on HIGH for 5 minutes, stirring twice. Leave to stand for 2–3 minutes.

4. Drain the spaghetti and place on a serving plate. Spoon over the bolognese sauce and serve at once.

TWO

1. Break the spaghetti in half and place in a deep bowl with the water and salt to taste. Cover and microwave on HIGH for 10 minutes, stirring once. Leave to stand, covered, for 5 minutes.

2. Place the beef, onion, garlic purée and pepper in a bowl. Microwave on HIGH for 3½–4 minutes, stirring once.

3. Add the tomato purée, tomatoes, Worcestershire sauce, oregano and salt and pepper to taste, blending well. Cover and microwave on HIGH for 10 minutes, stirring twice. Leave to stand for 2–3 minutes.

4. Drain the spaghetti and place on a serving plate. Spoon over the bolognese sauce and serve at once.

STUFFED BAKED ONIONS

Large, Spanish onions are very good for 'hollowing out' and stuffing with a savoury mixture.

ONE		TWO
1	**large Spanish onions, peeled**	2
5 ml/1 tsp	**oil**	10 ml/2 tsp
100 g/4 oz	**minced beef**	225 g/8 oz
7.5 ml/1½ tsp	**tomato purée**	15 ml/1 tbsp
25 g/1 oz	**clean mushrooms, chopped**	50 g/2 oz
5 ml/1 tsp	**flour**	10 ml/2 tsp
	pinch of dried mixed herbs	
	salt and freshly ground black pepper	
	parsley sprigs, to garnish	

ONE

1. Slice the top from the onion, remove the root end and discard. Place in a shallow dish and cover. Microwave on HIGH for 4–6 minutes until almost tender.

2. Scoop out the centre of the onion with a serrated teaspoon or a sharp knife and chop finely.

3. Place the oil, chopped onion and beef in a bowl. Microwave on HIGH for 3 minutes, stirring once.

4. Add the tomato purée, mushrooms, flour, herbs and salt and pepper to taste, blending well. Microwave on HIGH for 2 minutes, stirring once.

5. Spoon the beef mixture into the onion case, piling it high. Return to the dish, cover and microwave on HIGH for 2–3 minutes until the onion is tender. Serve hot, garnished with parsley sprigs.

TWO

1. Slice the tops from the onions, remove the root ends and discard. Place in a shallow dish and cover. Microwave on HIGH for 9–11 minutes until almost tender.

2. Scoop out the centres of the onions with a serrated teaspoon or a sharp knife and chop finely.

3. Place the oil, chopped onion and beef in a bowl. Microwave on HIGH for 5–6 minutes, stirring once.

4. Add the tomato purée, mushrooms, flour, herbs and salt and pepper to taste, blending well. Microwave on HIGH for 3–4 minutes, stirring once.

5. Spoon the beef mixture into the onion cases piling it high. Return to the baking dish, cover and microwave on HIGH for 4–6 minutes until the onion is tender. Serve hot, garnished with parsley sprigs.

CHILLI MINCED BEEF AND BEANS

Condensed oxtail soup makes a delicious thick savoury base for this Mexican inspired dish.

ONE		TWO
100 g/4 oz	**minced beef**	225 g/8 oz
½	**small onion, peeled and chopped**	1
5 ml/1 tsp	**chilli powder**	10 ml/2 tsp
½ × 225 g/8 oz	**can chopped tomatoes**	1 × 225 g/8 oz
¼ × 298 g/10 oz	**can condensed oxtail soup**	½ × 298 g/10 oz
50 g/2 oz	**cooked red kidney or butter beans**	100 g/4 oz
1	**small stick celery, scrubbed and chopped**	2

ONE

1. Place the beef and onion in a bowl. Cover and microwave on HIGH for 2 minutes. Break up with a fork and stir in the chilli powder, blending well.

2. Add the tomatoes and soup, blending well. Cover and microwave on HIGH for 5 minutes, stirring once.

3. Add the beans and celery, blending well. Cover and microwave on HIGH for 2 minutes, stirring once. Allow to stand for 3 minutes before serving with rice or corn chips.

TWO

1. Place the beef and onion in a bowl. Cover and microwave on HIGH for 3½–4 minutes. Break up with a fork and stir in the chilli powder, blending well.

2. Add the tomatoes and soup, blending well. Cover and microwave on HIGH for 10 minutes, stirring once.

3. Add the beans and celery, blending well. Cover and microwave on HIGH for 3–4 minutes, stirring once. Allow to stand for 3 minutes before serving with rice or corn chips.

KIDNEYS IN RED WINE

Tender lamb's kidneys make good and economical buying for 1 or 2. Always cook on the day of purchase or freeze until required. Serve with boiled rice.

ONE		TWO
15 g/½ oz	**butter**	20 g/¾ oz
3	**lamb's kidneys, skinned, cored and quartered**	6
½	**small onion, peeled and chopped**	1
75 g/3 oz	**button mushrooms, wiped and sliced**	175 g/6 oz
10 ml/2 tsp	**flour**	20 ml/4 tsp
	pinch of dried oregano	
2	**tomatoes, skinned, seeded and chopped**	3
50 ml/2 fl oz	**dry red wine**	100 ml/4 fl oz
	salt and freshly ground black pepper	
	parsley sprigs, to garnish	

ONE

1. Place the butter in a bowl and microwave on HIGH for ½ minute to melt. Add the kidney, onion and mushrooms, blending well. Cover and microwave on HIGH for 2–3 minutes, stirring once.

2. Add the flour, oregano and tomatoes, blending well. Gradually add the wine and salt and pepper to taste. Cover and microwave on HIGH for 1½–2 minutes, stirring three times, until the juices are thickened and the kidneys are tender.

3. Garnish with parsley sprigs and serve at once.

TWO

1. Place the butter in a bowl and microwave on HIGH for ¾ minute to melt. Add the kidney, onion and mushrooms, blending well. Cover and microwave on HIGH for 4–5 minutes, stirring once.

2. Add the flour, oregano and tomatoes, blending well. Gradually add the wine and salt and pepper to taste. Cover and microwave on HIGH for 3–3½ minutes, stirring three times, until the juices are thickened and the kidneys are tender.

3. Garnish with parsley sprigs and serve at once.

SAUSAGE PILAU

Sausages are endlessly versatile main meal ingredients and when combined with onion, rice, sweetcorn, beans and mushrooms make a worthy and hearty main course.

ONE		TWO
2	**pork sausages**	4
5 ml/1 tsp	**oil**	10 ml/2 tsp
½	**small onion, peeled and chopped**	1
25 g/1 oz	**long-grain rice**	50 g/2 oz
25 g/1 oz	**sweetcorn kernels**	50 g/2 oz
25 g/1 oz	**green beans**	50 g/2 oz
25 g/1 oz	**sliced mushrooms**	50 g/2 oz
5 ml/1 tsp	**Worcestershire sauce**	10 ml/2 tsp
	salt and freshly ground black pepper	
150 ml/¼ pint	**chicken stock**	300 ml/½ pint

ONE

1. Prick the sausages and place on a plate. Cover with absorbent kitchen towel and microwave on HIGH for 1½–2 minutes, turning over once. Cut into bite-sized pieces and set aside.

2. Place the oil and onion in a bowl. Cover and microwave on HIGH for 1 minute. Add the rice, cover and microwave on HIGH for 1 minute.

3. Add the sweetcorn, beans, mushrooms, Worcestershire sauce, salt and pepper to taste and stock, blending well. Cover and microwave on HIGH for 3 minutes. Reduce the power setting and microwave on MEDIUM for 12 minutes, stirring once. Add the sausages, blending well. Leave to stand, covered, for 5 minutes. Serve with a salad.

TWO

1. Prick the sausages and place on a plate. Cover with absorbent kitchen towel and microwave on HIGH for 3–3½ minutes, turning over once. Slice into bite-sized pieces and set aside.

2. Place the oil and onion in a bowl. Cover and microwave on HIGH for 1½ minutes. Add the rice, cover and microwave on HIGH for 1½ minutes.

3. Add the sweetcorn, beans, mushrooms, Worcestershire sauce, salt and pepper to taste and stock, blending well. Cover and microwave on HIGH for 3 minutes. Reduce the power setting and microwave on MEDIUM for 12 minutes, stirring once. Add the sausages, blending well. Leave to stand, covered, for 5 minutes. Serve with a salad.

LIVER AND BACON

Liver and bacon continues to be a good nutritious main meal when time is short – the microwave makes light work of this simple dish.

ONE		TWO
1 × 175 g/6 oz	**pieces of lamb's liver**	2 × 175 g/6 oz
7 g/¼ oz	**butter**	15 g/½ oz
	freshly ground black pepper	
	dash of lemon juice	
2	**rashers back bacon, rinded**	4

ONE

1. Place the liver in a shallow dish. Dot with the butter and sprinkle with the pepper and lemon juice. Microwave on HIGH for 1 minute. Turn over and microwave on HIGH for a further ½–¾ minute depending upon the thickness of the liver. Cover and leave to stand while cooking the bacon.

2. Place the bacon on a serving plate and cover with a sheet of absorbent kitchen towel. Microwave on HIGH for 2 minutes until cooked.

3. Serve the liver with the bacon slices.

TWO

1. Place the liver in a shallow dish. Dot with the butter and sprinkle with the pepper and lemon juice. Microwave on HIGH for 2 minutes. Turn over and microwave on HIGH for a further 1–1½ minutes depending upon the thickness of the liver. Cover and leave to stand while cooking the bacon.

2. Place the bacon on a serving plate and cover with a sheet of absorbent kitchen towel. Microwave on HIGH for 2½–3½ minutes until cooked.

3. Serve the liver with the bacon slices.

CHICKEN WITH MUSHROOM CREAM SAUCE

Canned soup makes a flavoursome base for a casserole or a sauce and has the added advantage that it doesn't need thickening. Here celery soup adds flavour to chicken joints.

ONE		TWO
7 g/¼ oz	**butter**	15 g/½ oz
1	**chicken joints, skinned**	2
10 ml/2 tsp	**dry sherry**	20 ml/4 tsp
75 ml/5 tbsp	**cream of celery soup**	150 ml/¼ pint
25 g/1 oz	**mushrooms, sliced**	50 g/2 oz
45 ml/3 tbsp	**single cream**	75 ml/5 tbsp
	salt and freshly ground black pepper	

ONE

1. Place the butter in a dish and microwave on HIGH for ½ minute to melt. Add the chicken and microwave on HIGH for 1½–2 minutes, turning over once.

2. Add the sherry and soup, blending well. Cover and microwave on HIGH for 7 minutes. Add the mushrooms and microwave for 1 minute.

3. Stir in the cream and salt and pepper to taste, blending well. Cover and allow to stand for 3 minutes before serving.

TWO

1. Place the butter in a dish and microwave on HIGH for ¾ minute to melt. Add the chicken and microwave on HIGH for 3–4 minutes, turning over once.
2. Add the sherry and soup, blending well. Cover and microwave on HIGH for 14 minutes. Add the mushrooms and microwave for 2 minutes.
3. Stir in the cream and salt and pepper to taste, blending well. Cover and allow to stand for 3 minutes before serving.

CHICKEN LIVERS WITH GRAPES

Juicy, tender, succulent and pink, chicken livers cook extra fast in the microwave to make a speedy dish. However, do remember to prick them before cooking so that they do not burst.

ONE		TWO
15 g/½ oz	**butter**	25 g/1 oz
175 g/6 oz	**chicken livers, trimmed and halved**	350 g/12 oz
5 ml/1 tsp	**wholegrain mustard**	10 ml/2 tsp
15–30 ml/1–2 tbsp	**Marsala or stock**	45–60 ml/ 3–4 tbsp
	salt and freshly ground black pepper	
75 g/3 oz	**green grapes, halved and seeded**	175 g/6 oz

ONE

1. Place the butter in a small cooking dish and microwave on HIGH for ½ minute.

2. Add the chicken livers and microwave on HIGH for 2 minutes, stirring once.

3. Add the mustard, Marsala or stock, salt and pepper to taste and grapes, blending well. Microwave on HIGH for a further 1½–2 minutes until cooked but the chicken livers are still pink.

4. Serve hot with triangles of toast.

TWO

1. Place the butter in a small cooking dish and microwave on HIGH for 1 minute.

2. Add the chicken livers and microwave on HIGH for 3 minutes, stirring once.

3. Add the mustard, Marsala or stock, salt and pepper to taste and grapes, blending well. Microwave on HIGH for a further 2½–3 minutes, until cooked but the chicken livers are still pink.

4. Serve hot with triangles of toast.

See photograph on page 81

CHICKEN BEAN BAKE

A nourishing gratin style dish, Chicken Bean Bake can be made using leftover chicken or turkey or a bought ready-cooked portion of the same. Serve with a crisp salad.

ONE		TWO
150 ml/¼ pint	**hot White Sauce (see page 95)**	300 ml/½ pint
75 g/3 oz	**cooked chicken, chopped**	175 g/6 oz
100 g/4 oz	**canned baked beans in tomato sauce**	225 g/8 oz
25 g/1 oz	**pasta twists, cooked**	50 g/2 oz
25 g/1 oz	**Cheddar cheese, grated**	50 g/2 oz
	salt and freshly ground black pepper	
1 small	**tomato, sliced**	1 large
7 g/¼ oz	**flaked almonds**	15 g/½ oz

ONE

1. Mix the white sauce with the chicken, blending well.

2. Add the beans, cooked pasta and three-quarters of the cheese, blending well. Season to taste with salt and pepper and place in a shallow heatproof dish.

3. Arrange the tomato slices on top, sprinkle with the remaining cheese and scatter over the almonds. Microwave on HIGH for 2–3 minutes. Brown under a preheated grill if liked. Serve hot.

TWO

1. Mix the white sauce with the chicken, blending well.

2. Add the beans, cooked pasta and three-quarters of the cheese, blending well. Season to taste with salt and pepper and place in a shallow heatproof dish.

3. Arrange the tomato slices on top, sprinkle with the remaining cheese and scatter over the almonds. Microwave on HIGH for 4–5 minutes. Brown under a preheated grill if liked. Serve hot.

COOK'S TIP

This dish is a good combination of leftovers and storecupboard standbys.

STUFFED ROAST POUSSINS

Tender, sweet and succulent baby chickens, stuffed with a ham and oat stuffing, make delicious eating when roasted and basted with a herby butter.

ONE		TWO
1	**poussins, cleaned**	2
1	**recipe Ham Oat Stuffing (see page 103)**	1
15 g/½ oz	**butter**	25 g/1 oz
15 ml/1 tbsp	**chopped fresh mixed herbs**	30 ml/2 tbsp
	watercress sprigs, to garnish	

ONE

1. Stuff the poussin with the stuffing and truss with string to make a neat shape.

2. Preheat a browning dish on HIGH for 8 minutes or according to the manufacturer's instructions.

3. Add half of the butter and swirl to coat the base of the dish. Add the poussin, breast side down, and turn quickly to brown the breast on each side. Remove from the dish, dot the breast with the remaining butter and sprinkle with the herbs. Place in a small roasting bag on an upturned saucer in a dish.

4. Reduce the power setting and microwave on MEDIUM for 9–11 minutes. Leave to stand, covered, for 10 minutes. Serve hot garnished with watercress.

TWO

1. Stuff the poussins with the stuffing and truss with string to make a neat shape.

2. Preheat a browning dish on HIGH for 8 minutes or according to the manufacturer's instructions.

3. Add half of the butter and swirl to coat the base of the dish. Add the poussins, breast side down, and turn quickly to brown the breasts on each side. Remove, dot each breast with the remaining butter and sprinkle with the herbs. Place in a medium roasting bag on an upturned saucer in a dish.

4. Reduce the power setting and microwave on MEDIUM for 18–20 minutes. Leave to stand, covered, for 10 minutes. Serve hot garnished with watercress.

SPICED CHICKEN AND MANGO

This Eastern spiced dish relies upon the cunning combination of a few spices with chicken, tomatoes and mango. Serve with Creamed Coconut and Pine Nut Rice (see page 94).

ONE		TWO
2.5 ml/½ tsp	**oil**	5 ml/1 tsp
½	**large onion, peeled and sliced**	1
¼	**red pepper, cored, seeded and sliced**	½
¼	**green pepper, cored, seeded and sliced**	½
pinch	**ground ginger**	1.25 ml/¼ tsp
5 ml/1 tsp	**ground coriander**	7.5 ml/1½ tsp
7.5 ml/1½ tsp	**garam masala**	15 ml/1 tbsp
2.5 ml/½ tsp	**ground cumin**	5 ml/1 tsp
2.5 ml/½ tsp	**finely grated lemon rind**	5 ml/1 tsp
1 × 225 g/8 oz	**can chopped tomatoes**	1 × 397 g/14 oz
	salt and freshly ground black pepper	
150 g/5 oz	**cooked chicken, skinned and cut into bite-sized pieces**	275 g/10 oz
½	**ripe mango, peeled, stoned and cubed**	1
45 ml/3 tbsp	**set natural yogurt**	75 ml/5 tbsp
2.5 ml/½ tsp	**mint sauce**	5 ml/1 tsp
	chopped fresh coriander, to garnish	

ONE

1. Place the oil, onion, peppers, ginger, ground coriander, garam masala and cumin in a bowl. Cover and microwave on HIGH for 2 minutes, stirring once.

2. Add the lemon rind, tomatoes and salt and pepper to taste, blending well. Cover and microwave on HIGH for 2 minutes, stirring once.

3. Add the chicken and fresh mango, blending well. Cover, reduce the power setting and microwave on MEDIUM for 5 minutes, stirring twice.

4. Meanwhile blend the yogurt with the mint sauce.

5. Serve hot drizzled with minted yogurt and garnished with chopped coriander.

TWO

1. Place the oil, onion, peppers, ginger, ground coriander, garam masala and cumin in a bowl. Cover and microwave on HIGH for 4 minutes, stirring once.

2. Add the lemon rind, tomatoes and salt and pepper to taste, blending well. Cover and microwave on HIGH for 2–3 minutes, stirring once.

3. Add the chicken and fresh mangos, blending well. Cover, reduce the power setting and microwave on MEDIUM for 10 minutes, stirring twice.

4. Meanwhile blend the yogurt with the mint sauce.

5. Serve hot drizzled with minted yogurt and garnished with chopped coriander.

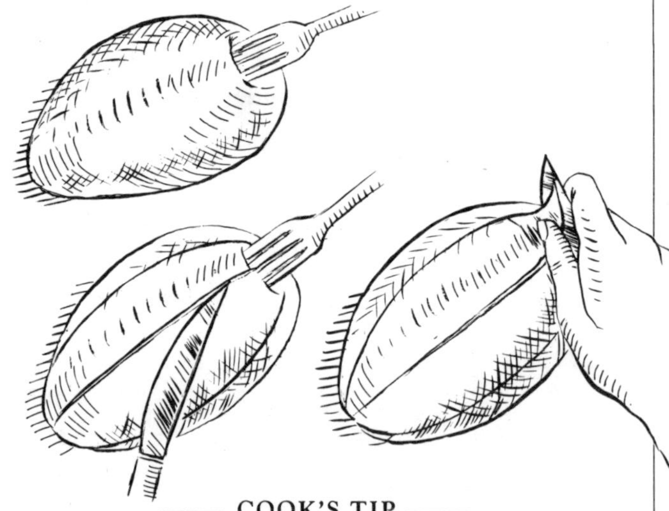

COOK'S TIP

Peeling a mango can be quite an awesome task – here is the simplest and most rewarding way. Spear one end of the mango with a fork. Using the fork to hold the mango, cut the fruit's skin lengthways with a sharp knife to divide into 4 sections. Grip each section of skin between your thumb and the knife and gently pull away to strip off the skin.

See photograph on page 81

TURKEY BREAST PARCELS

This is the microwave answer to cooking meat in a foil parcel or 'papillote', where the foil is replaced by a plastic roast or cook-bag. Use chicken fillets or breasts if turkey breast escalopes are unavailable.

ONE		TWO
1 × 225 g/8 oz	**turkey breast escalopes**	2 × 225 g/8 oz
7 g/¼ oz	**butter**	15 g/½ oz
1	**tomatoes, skinned and coarsely chopped**	2
1	**sticks celery, scrubbed and finely sliced**	2
25 g/1 oz	**sweetcorn kernels**	50 g/2 oz
25 g/1 oz	**cooked ham, chopped**	50 g/2 oz
	salt and freshly ground black pepper	
30 ml/2 tbsp	**chicken stock**	60 ml/4 tbsp
	chopped fresh parsley, to garnish	

ONE

1. Rub the turkey with the butter and place in a small roast or cook bag.

2. Mix the tomatoes with the celery, sweetcorn, ham and salt and pepper to taste, blending well. Spoon on top of the turkey. Add the stock to the bag, seal loosely with an elastic band, plastic tie or string.

3. Microwave on HIGH for 2 minutes. Reduce the power setting to MEDIUM and cook for a further 5–7 minutes until tender.

4. Transfer to a serving plate, but open the bag (taking care as the steam released can burn) and lift out the turkey and vegetable mixture.

5. Garnish with chopped parsley and serve hot.

TWO

1. Rub the turkey with the butter and place in a small roast or cook bag.

2. Mix the tomatoes with the celery, sweetcorn, ham and salt and pepper to taste, blending well. Spoon on top of the turkey. Add the stock to the bag, seal loosely with an elastic band, plastic tie or string.

3. Microwave on HIGH for 3½ minutes. Reduce the power setting on MEDIUM and cook for a further 8–10 minutes until tender.

4. Transfer to a serving plate, cut open the bag (taking care as the steam released can burn) and lift out the turkey and vegetable mixture.

5. Garnish with chopped parsley and serve hot.

See photograph on page 48

TURKEY RISOTTO

A favourite rice recipe with something for everyone – turkey, peppers, pineapple and raisins. Good for using up leftover meat like turkey, chicken or duck.

ONE		TWO
25 g/1 oz	**butter**	50 g/2 oz
½	**large onion, peeled and chopped**	1
½	**green pepper, cored, seeded and chopped**	1
½	**stick celery, scrubbed and chopped**	1
75 g/3 oz	**long-grain rice**	175 g/6 oz
150 ml/¼ pint	**boiling chicken stock**	300 ml/½ pint
	salt and freshly ground black pepper	
7.5 ml/1½ tsp	**raisins**	15 ml/1 tbsp
75 g/3 oz	**cooked turkey, skinned and chopped**	175 g/6 oz
1	**pineapple rings, diced**	2

ONE

1. Place the butter, onion, pepper and celery in a bowl. Cover and microwave on HIGH for 3–4 minutes until tender, stirring once.

2. Add the rice, stock and salt and pepper to taste. Cover and microwave on HIGH for 3 minutes, stirring once. Reduce the power setting and microwave on MEDIUM for 12 minutes.

3. Add the raisins, turkey and pineapple, blending well. Cover and allow to stand for 5 minutes before serving.

TWO

1. Place the butter, onion, pepper and celery in a bowl. Cover and microwave on HIGH for 5–7 minutes until tender, stirring once.

2. Add the rice, stock and salt and pepper to taste. Cover and microwave on HIGH for 3 minutes, stirring once. Reduce the power setting and microwave on MEDIUM for 12 minutes.

3. Add the raisins, turkey and pineapple, blending well. Cover and allow to stand for 5 minutes before serving.

CHINESE DUCK

Duck breasts are often available in supermarkets ready trimmed and prepared and are deliciously easy and quick to cook in the microwave.

ONE		TWO
1 × 175 g/6 oz	**duck breasts**	2 × 175 g/6 oz
	Marinade and Baste:	
7.5 ml/1½ tsp	**soy sauce**	15 ml/1 tbsp
20 ml/4 tsp	**clear honey**	40 ml/8 tsp
20 ml/4 tsp	**sesame oil**	40 ml/8 tsp
30 ml/2 tbsp	**dry sherry or orange juice**	60 ml/4 tbsp
2.5 ml/½ tsp	**finely chopped fresh root ginger**	5 ml/1 tsp
2.5 ml/½ tsp	**finely grated orange rind**	5 ml/1 tsp
½	**small onion, peeled and chopped**	1
	pinch of Chinese 5 spice powder	
	freshly ground black pepper	
	spring onion curls, to garnish	

ONE

1. Using a sharp knife, make diagonal cuts across the skin of the duck to make a diamond optional cut pattern.

2. Mix the soy sauce with the honey, oil, sherry or orange juice, ginger, orange rind, onion, Chinese 5 spice powder and black pepper to taste, blending well. Spoon over the duck and leave to marinate for 2–4 hours, turning occasionally.

3. Remove the duck from the marinade with a slotted spoon and place on a roasting rack. Brush with a little of the marinade and microwave on MEDIUM for 6–8 minutes, brushing with the marinade twice and turning over once during cooking. Allow to stand for 3–5 minutes.

4. If a crisp skin is preferred quickly brown the duck to crisp under a preheated grill before serving. Carve into thick slices and arrange on a warmed serving plate.

5. Garnish with spring onion curls and serve at once with a green vegetable.

TWO

1. Using a sharp knife, make diagonal cuts across the surface skin of the duck to make a diamond or chequered pattern.

2. Mix the soy sauce with the honey, oil, sherry or orange juice, ginger, orange rind, onion, Chinese 5 spice powder and black pepper to taste, blending well. Spoon over the duck and leave to marinate for 2–4 hours, turning occasionally.

3. Remove the duck from the marinade with a slotted spoon and place on a roasting rack. Brush with a little of the marinade and microwave on MEDIUM for 12–16 minutes, brushing with the marinade twice and turning over once during cooking. Allow to stand for 3–5 minutes.

4. If a crisp skin is preferred quickly brown the duck to crisp under a preheated grill. Carve into thick slices and arrange on a warmed serving plate.

5. Garnish with spring onion curls and serve at once with a green vegetable.

COOK'S TIP

If duck breasts are unavailable use chicken or turkey breasts instead.

HIGH FIBRE PANCAKE PARCELS

It isn't possible to make traditional pancakes in the microwave but well worth the effort of making a few extra traditional ones which can be frozen for later use. In this recipe pancakes are stuffed with beans, corn and cheese then reheated in minutes in the microwave to make a nourishing, high fibre main course.

ONE		TWO
½ × 213 g 7½ oz can	**baked beans in tomato sauce**	1 × 213 g 7½ oz can
½ × 198 g 7 oz can	**corn with sweet peppers, drained**	1 × 198 g 7 oz can
50 g/2 oz	**Cheddar cheese, grated**	100 g/4 oz
2	**wholewheat pancakes**	4
	watercress sprigs, to garnish	

ONE

1. Mix the beans with the corn and half of the cheese, blending well.

2. Divide the mixture between the pancakes, fold into parcels and place in a greased shallow dish. Sprinkle with the remaining cheese.

3. Microwave on HIGH for 2–3½ minutes until hot and bubbly. Brown under a preheated grill, if liked. Serve at once garnished with watercress sprigs.

TWO

1. Mix the beans with the corn and half of the cheese, blending well.

2. Divide the mixture between the pancakes, fold into parcels and place in a greased shallow dish. Sprinkle with the remaining cheese.

3. Microwave on HIGH for 3½–5 minutes until hot and bubbly. Brown under a preheated grill if liked. Serve at once garnished with watercress sprigs.

QUICK BEAN CASSOULET

Look out for the new canned cassoulet beans in sauce when making this dish – if unavailable use baked beans in tomato sauce instead.

ONE		TWO
15 g/½ oz	**butter**	25 g/1 oz
50 g/2 oz	**mushrooms sliced**	100 g/4 oz
2	**tomatoes, skinned, seeded and chopped**	4
100 g/4 oz	**canned cassoulet beans**	225 g/8 oz
	salt and freshly ground black pepper	
	pinch of mixed dried herbs	
25 g/1 oz	**wholemeal breadcrumbs or Crispy Croûtons (see page 94)**	50 g/2 oz

ONE

1. Place the butter and mushrooms in a serving dish. Microwave on HIGH for 1 minute, stirring once.

2. Add the tomatoes, cassoulet beans, salt and pepper to taste and herbs, blending well. Cover and microwave on HIGH for 3 minutes, stirring once.

3. Sprinkle with the breadcrumbs or croûtons. Brown under a preheated grill, if liked. Serve at once with crusty bread or a salad.

TWO

1. Place the butter and mushrooms in a serving dish. Microwave on HIGH for 1½ minutes, stirring once.

2. Add the tomatoes, cassoulet beans, salt and pepper to taste and herbs, blending well. Cover and microwave on HIGH for 6 minutes, stirring once.

3. Sprinkle with the breadcrumbs or croûtons. Brown under a preheated grill if liked. Serve at once with crusty bread or a salad.

COOK'S TIP

The microwave will speedily help with peeling tomatoes for cooked dishes. Pierce the skin and place on a plate. Microwave on HIGH for 1–2 minutes, depending on number, then peel or strip the skin away easily.

CORN AND VEGETABLE CURRY

This colourful vegetable curry is just the dish to serve when a vegetarian meal is requested. Serve with nutty brown rice and a crisp salad.

ONE		TWO
75 g/3 oz	**cauliflower florets**	175 g/6 oz
50 g/2 oz	**carrots, peeled and sliced**	100 g/4 oz
25 g/1 oz	**green beans, topped, tailed and cut into 2.5 cm/1 inch lengths**	50 g/2 oz
30 ml/2 tbsp	**water**	60 ml/4 tbsp
10 ml/2 tsp	**oil**	20 ml/4 tsp
½	**small onion, peeled and sliced**	1
½	**garlic clove, peeled and crushed**	1
5 ml/1 tsp	**garam masala**	10 ml/2 tsp
1.25 ml/¼ tsp	**ground paprika**	2.5 ml/½ tsp
	pinch of cayenne pepper	
3.75 ml/¾ tsp	**wholewheat flour**	7.5 ml/1½ tsp
75 ml/5 tbsp	**vegetable stock**	150 ml/¼ pint
15 ml/1 tbsp	**single cream or top of the milk**	30 ml/2 tbsp
7.5 ml/3 tsp	**chopped fresh coriander**	15 ml/1 tbsp
65 g/2½ oz	**canned sweetcorn kernels**	150 g/5 oz
50 g/2 oz	**cooked or canned chick peas**	100 g/4 oz

ONE

1. Place the cauliflower florets, carrots, beans and water in a bowl. Cover and microwave on HIGH for 6 minutes until tender, stirring once.

2. Place the oil, onion and garlic in a bowl. Microwave on HIGH for 2 minutes.

3. Add the garam masala, paprika and cayenne pepper, blending well. Microwave on HIGH for ½ minute.

4. Stir in the flour then gradually add the stock, blending well. Microwave on HIGH for 2 minutes, stirring three times until boiling, smooth and thickened.

5. Add the cream or milk, coriander, sweetcorn, chick peas and the cooked vegetables blending well. Reduce the power setting and microwave on MEDIUM for 4 minutes. Serve hot with brown rice.

TWO

1. Place the cauliflower florets, carrots, beans and water in a bowl. Cover and microwave on HIGH for 10–12 minutes until tender, stirring once.

2. Place the oil, onion and garlic in a bowl. Microwave on HIGH for 3–4 minutes.

3. Add the garam masala, paprika and cayenne pepper, blending well. Microwave on HIGH for 1 minute.

4. Stir in the flour then gradually add the stock, blending well. Microwave on HIGH for 3–4 minutes, stirring three times until boiling, smooth and thickened.

5. Add the cream or milk, coriander, sweetcorn, chick peas and the cooked vegetables, blending well. Reduce the power setting and microwave on MEDIUM for 7–8 minutes, serve hot with brown rice.

WHOLEWHEAT SPAGHETTI WITH SPINACH

Rich, creamy and wholesome, this delicious pasta dish belies its humble ingredients. When fresh spinach is unavailable use frozen leaf spinach instead.

ONE		TWO
50 g/2 oz	**dried wholewheat spaghetti**	100 g/4 oz
500 ml/14 fl oz	**boiling water**	1 litre/1¾ pints
	salt	
100 g/4 oz	**spinach leaves**	225 g/8 oz
15 g/½ oz	**savoury butter with black pepper**	25 g/1 oz
	pinch of ground nutmeg	
1 small	**egg**	1 large
50 ml/2 fl oz	**double cream**	100 ml/4 fl oz
20 g/¾ oz	**Cheddar cheese, grated**	40 g/1½ oz
2.5 ml/½ tsp	**toasted sesame seeds**	5 ml/1 tsp

ONE

1. Break the spaghetti in half and place in a deep bowl with the water and salt to taste. Cover and microwave on HIGH for 10 minutes, stirring once. Leave to stand, covered, for 5 minutes until tender.

2. Meanwhile, wash the spinach leaves and place in a bowl with a pinch of salt. Cover and microwave on HIGH for 2–3 minutes, shaking the bowl twice. Drain and stir in the savoury butter and nutmeg.

3. Beat the egg with the cream, cheese and a pinch of salt.

4. Drain the spaghetti and return to the bowl. Stir in the egg mixture and toss the spaghetti thoroughly. Microwave on HIGH for ½ minute.

5. Spoon onto a heated serving dish, sprinkle with the sesame seeds and top with the buttered spinach. Serve at once.

TWO

1. Break the spaghetti in half and place in a deep bowl with the water and salt to taste. Cover and microwave on HIGH for 10 minutes. Leave to stand, covered, for 5 minutes.

2. Meanwhile, wash the spinach leaves and place in a bowl with a pinch of salt. Cover and microwave on HIGH for 3–4 minutes, shaking the bowl twice. Drain and stir in the savoury butter and nutmeg.

3. Beat the egg with the cream, cheese and a pinch of salt.

4. Drain the spaghetti and return to the bowl. Stir in the egg mixture and toss the spaghetti thoroughly. Microwave on HIGH for ¾ minute.

5. Spoon onto a heated serving dish, sprinkle with the sesame seeds and top with the buttered spinach. Serve at once.

SPAGHETTI WITH NAPOLITAN SAUCE

Fresh wholewheat spaghetti is now available in many supermarkets and combined with this fresh tomato herb sauce makes a hearty, economical and wholesome meat-free main course.

ONE		TWO
100 g/4 oz	**fresh wholewheat spaghetti**	225 g/8 oz
600 ml/1 pint	**herb stock**	1.2 litres/2 pints
7.5 ml/1½ tsp	**olive oil**	15 ml/1 tbsp
½	**small onion, peeled and chopped**	1
1 small	**garlic clove, peeled and crushed**	1 large
100 g/4 oz	**tomatoes, skinned and chopped**	225 g/8 oz
2.5 ml/½ tsp	**chopped fresh mixed herbs**	5 ml/1 tsp
	salt and freshly ground black pepper	
7 g/¼ oz	**butter**	15 g/½ oz
	grated Parmesan cheese, to serve	

ONE

1. Place the fresh wholewheat spaghetti in a large shallow rectangular heatproof dish or casserole. Add the boiling stock, cover and microwave on HIGH for 4 minutes. Leave to stand, covered, while preparing the sauce.

2. Place the oil in a bowl with the onion and garlic. Cover and microwave on HIGH for 1 minute.

3. Stir in the tomatoes, herbs and salt and pepper to taste, blending well. Cover and microwave on HIGH for 1–1½ minutes, stirring once.

4. Drain the spaghetti and toss in the butter. Place on a serving dish and spoon over the sauce. Serve at once sprinkled with grated Parmesan cheese.

TWO

1. Place the fresh wholewheat spaghetti in a large shallow rectangular heatproof dish or casserole. Add the boiling stock, cover and microwave on HIGH for 4 minutes. Leave to stand, covered, while preparing the sauce.

2. Place the oil in a bowl with the onion and garlic. Cover and microwave on HIGH for 2 minutes.

3. Stir in the tomatoes, herbs and salt and pepper to taste, blending well. Cover and microwave on HIGH for 2–3 minutes, stirring once.

4. Drain the spaghetti and toss in the butter. Place on a serving dish and spoon over the sauce. Serve at once sprinkled with grated Parmesan cheese.

STUFFED REDSKINS

Large ripe, hand-sized beef tomatoes seem intended for stuffing. In this recipe they are filled fit-to-burst with rice, curried beans and mushrooms. Serve with a simple salad.

ONE		TWO
5 ml/1 tsp	**oil**	10 ml/2 tsp
½	**small onion, peeled and chopped**	1
50 g/2 oz	**cooked rice**	100 g/4 oz
5 ml/1 tsp	**tomato purée**	10 ml/2 tsp
25 g/1 oz	**button mushrooms, wiped and chopped**	50 g/2 oz
	salt and freshly ground black pepper	
1	**large beef tomatoes**	2
1 × 50–75 g/2–3 oz	**canned curried beans**	1 × 100–175 g/4–6 oz
	pinch of dried mixed herbs	

ONE

1. Place the oil and onion in a bowl. Cover and microwave on HIGH for 1½ minutes. Add the rice, blending well.

2. Add the tomato purée, mushrooms and salt and pepper to taste, blending well. Cover and microwave on HIGH for 2 minutes, stirring once.

3. Meanwhile, using a serrated knife, cut off and reserve the top of the tomato. Carefully scoop out and discard the seeds.

4. Mix the rice with the curried beans and herbs, blending well. Spoon into the tomato case using the reserved top to make a lid and place in a shallow dish.

5. Reduce the power setting and microwave on MEDIUM for 2–3 minutes until hot, bubbly and cooked. Serve at once with a salad.

TWO

1. Place the oil and onion in a bowl. Cover and microwave on HIGH for 2 minutes. Add the rice, blending well.

2. Add the tomato purée, mushrooms and salt and pepper to taste, blending well. Cover and microwave on HIGH for 3–4 minutes, stirring once.

3. Meanwhile, using a serrated knife, cut off and reserve the tops of the tomatoes. Carefully scoop out and discard the seeds.

4. Mix the rice with the curried beans and herbs, blending well. Spoon into the tomato cases, use the reserved tops to make lids and place in a shallow dish.

5. Reduce the power setting and microwave on MEDIUM for 3–4 minutes until hot, bubbly and cooked. Serve at once with a salad.

STUFFED EGGS FLORENTINE

Stuffed hard-boiled eggs nesting on a bed of leaf spinach and topped with a savoury cheese sauce makes a delicious and economical main meal. Serve with fingers of warm toast.

ONE		TWO
100 g/4 oz	**frozen leaf spinach**	225 g/8 oz
	pinch of ground nutmeg	
2	**hard-boiled eggs, shelled and halved lengthwise**	4
25 g/1 oz	**butter**	50 g/2 oz
15 g/½ oz	**chopped cooked mushrooms**	25 g/1 oz
5 ml/1 tsp	**chopped fresh parsley**	10 ml/2tsp
150 ml/¼ pint	**hot Cheese Sauce (see page 95)**	300 ml/½ pint

ONE

1. Place the spinach in a small gratin dish. Sprinkle with a little ground nutmeg. Cover and microwave on HIGH for 3–4 minutes.

2. Meanwhile, remove the yolks from the eggs and

mix with the butter, mushrooms and parsley. Spoon the mixture back into the egg whites and sandwich together. Place on top of the spinach.

3. Pour over the sauce and microwave on HIGH for 1 minute to reheat. Brown under a preheated grill if liked. Serve at once.

TWO

1. Place the spinach in a small gratin dish. Sprinkle with a little ground nutmeg. Cover and microwave on HIGH for 7–8 minutes.

2. Meanwhile, remove the yolks from the eggs and mix with the butter, mushrooms and parsley. Spoon the mixture back into the egg whites and sandwich together. Place on top of the spinach.

2. Pour over the sauce and microwave on HIGH for 1½–2 minutes to reheat. Brown under a preheated grill if liked. Serve at once.

COOK'S TIP

Frozen spinach is an ideal vegetable to cook in the microwave both as a vegetable accompaniment and as part of a cooked dish. It is much quicker and easier to use than fresh spinach.

SPANISH OMELETTE

A main-course omelette cooked with onion, pepper, tomatoes and potato. Serve with a seasonal green salad and crusty bread.

ONE		TWO
½	**medium onion, peeled and finely chopped**	1
½	**small green pepper, cored, seeded and chopped**	1
½	**tomato, skinned, seeded and chopped**	1
20 g/¾ oz	**butter**	40 g/1½ oz
½	**large cooked potato, diced**	1
2	**eggs, beaten**	4
20 ml/4 tsp	**milk**	45 ml/3 tbsp
	salt and freshly ground black pepper	

ONE

1. Place the onion, pepper, tomato and 15 g/½ oz of the butter in a bowl. Cover and microwave on HIGH for 2 minutes. Add the potato, blending well.

2. Mix the eggs with the milk and salt and pepper to taste, blending well.

3. Place the remaining butter in a 15–18 cm/ 6–7 inch pie plate and microwave on HIGH for ½ minute to melt. Swirl the butter over the plate to coat.

4. Mix the egg mixture with the vegetable mixture and pour into the plate. Cover with pierced cling film and microwave on HIGH for 1 minute. Using a fork, move the cooked egg from the edge of the dish to the centre. Re-cover and microwave on HIGH for a further 1–1½ minutes. Allow to stand for 2 minutes until set. Serve at once.

TWO

1. Place the onion, pepper, tomato and 25 g/1 oz of the butter in a bowl. Cover and microwave on HIGH for 3 minutes. Add the potato, blending well.

2. Mix the eggs with the milk and salt and pepper to taste, blending well.

3. Place the remaining butter in a 25 cm/10 inch pie plate and microwave on HIGH for ¾–1 minute to melt. Swirl the butter over the plate to coat.

4. Mix the egg mixture with the vegetable mixture and pour into the plate. Cover with pierced cling film and microwave on HIGH for 1½–2 minutes. Using a fork, move the cooked egg from the edge of the dish to the centre. Re-cover and microwave on HIGH for a further 1½–2¼ minutes. Allow to stand for 2 minutes until set. Serve at once.

SAVE AND SAVOUR

Use any leftover ingredients for this Spanish Omelette but make sure that they are chopped evenly and neatly.

Vegetables, Salads & Side Dishes

CABBAGE IN SOURED CREAM MUSHROOM SAUCE

Crunchy white cabbage served with a tangy mushroom sauce is delicious with almost any roast meat or game.

ONE		TWO
100 g/4 oz	**white cabbage, cut into small wedges**	225 g/8 oz
10 ml/2 tsp	**water**	20 ml/4 tsp
1	**recipe hot Soured Cream Mushroom Sauce (see page 98)**	1

ONE

1. Place the cabbage and water in a bowl. Cover and microwave on HIGH for 2½–3½ minutes until tender, stirring gently once.

2. Drain thoroughly. Spoon over the hot sauce and microwave on HIGH for ½ minute. Serve hot.

TWO

1. Place the cabbage and water in a bowl. Cover and microwave on HIGH for 5–5½ minutes until tender, stirring gently once.

2. Drain thoroughly. Spoon over the hot sauce and microwave on HIGH for ¾ minute. Serve hot.

FANTAIL LEMON COURGETTES

These sliced and fanned courgettes look stunning and are very easy to do. Take care not to damage them during cooking when stirring or re-arranging.

ONE		TWO
2	**medium courgettes**	4
7 g/¼ oz	**butter**	15 g/½ oz
2.5 ml/½ tsp	**finely grated lemon rind**	5 ml/1 tsp
	salt and freshly ground white pepper	

ONE

1. Top and tail the courgettes, then thinly slice from one end almost to the other to make several thin

layers. Gently prise the layers apart and open out to make a fan shape.

2. Place in a shallow dish, dot with the butter, sprinkle with the lemon rind and season with salt and pepper to taste. Cover and microwave on HIGH for 1½–2 minutes, stirring or re-arranging once.

TWO

1. Top and tail the courgettes then thinly slice from one end almost to the other to make several thin layers. Gently prise the layers apart and open out to make a fan shape.

2. Place in a shallow dish, dot with the butter, sprinkle with the lemon rind and season with salt and pepper to taste. Cover and microwave on HIGH for 3–4 minutes, stirring or re-arranging once.

CIDERED RED CABBAGE AND APPLE

A family favourite that I first tasted at Marden Fruit Show in Kent where top apple growers meet in friendly rivalry to compete for the best fruit awards.

ONE		TWO
150 g/5 oz	**red cabbage, shredded**	275 g/10 oz
7.5 ml/1½ tsp	**cider or apple juice**	15 ml/1 tbsp
½	**large cooking apple, peeled, cored and finely sliced**	1
	pinch of ground cloves	
2.5 ml/½ tsp	**cider vinegar**	5 ml/1 tsp
2.5 ml/½ tsp	**brown sugar**	5 ml/1 tsp
2.5 ml/½ tsp	**redcurrant or quince jelly**	5 ml/1 tsp
7 g/¼ oz	**butter**	15 g/½ oz

ONE

1. Place the cabbage, cider or apple juice and apple in a bowl. Cover and microwave on HIGH for 4–5 minutes, stirring once.

2. Add the cloves, cider vinegar, sugar, jelly and butter, blending well. Cover and microwave on HIGH for ¾–1 minute, stirring once. Serve hot.

TWO

1. Place the cabbage, cider or apple juice and apple in a bowl. Cover and microwave on HIGH for 8–9 minutes, stirring once.

2. Add the cloves, cider vinegar, sugar, jelly and butter, blending well. Cover and microwave on HIGH for 1–1½ minutes, stirring once. Serve hot.

FREEZABILITY

Cidered Red Cabbage and Apple will freeze well for up to 3 months. Defrost and reheat on HIGH for 4 minutes (for one) and 8 minutes (for two), stirring once.

BUTTERY LEMON CABBAGE

Crisp and flavoursome, simple white cabbage is lifted from the humble to the luxury class when cooked with lemon and butter.

ONE		TWO
100 g/4 oz	**white cabbage, finely shredded**	225 g/8 oz
2.5 ml/½ tsp	**finely grated lemon rind**	5 ml/1 tsp
10 ml/2 tsp	**lemon juice**	20 ml/4 tsp
15 g/½ oz	**butter**	25 g/1 oz
30 ml/2 tbsp	**chicken stock**	60 ml/4 tbsp
	salt and freshly ground black pepper	

ONE

1. Place the cabbage, lemon rind, lemon juice, butter, stock and salt and pepper to taste in a bowl.

2. Cover and microwave on HIGH for 2½–3½ minutes until tender, stirring once. Leave to stand for 3 minutes before serving.

TWO

1. Place the cabbage, lemon rind, lemon juice, butter, stock and salt and pepper to taste in a bowl.

2. Cover and microwave on HIGH for 5–5½ minutes until tender, stirring once. Leave to stand for 3 minutes before serving.

RATATOUILLE

Colourful, exotic and flavoursome ratatouille is delicious served with pork or poultry. Alternatively serve chilled as a starter with crusty bread.

ONE		TWO
5 ml/1 tsp	**oil**	10 ml/2 tsp
½	**small onion, peeled and chopped**	1
½	**garlic clove, peeled and crushed**	1
½	**green pepper, cored, seeded and sliced**	1
75 g/3 oz	**tomatoes, skinned and sliced**	175 g/6 oz
100 g/4 oz	**courgettes, topped, tailed and sliced**	225 g/8 oz
15 g/½ oz	**mushrooms, wiped and chopped**	25 g/1 oz
1.25 ml/¼ tsp	**dried thyme**	2.5 ml/½ tsp
7.5 ml/1½ tsp	**tomato purée**	15 ml/1 tbsp
	salt and freshly ground black pepper	

ONE

1. Place the oil, onion, garlic and green pepper in a bowl. Cover and microwave on HIGH for 2½ minutes, stirring once.

2. Add the tomatoes, courgettes, mushrooms, thyme, tomato purée and salt and pepper to taste, blending well. Cover and microwave on HIGH for 4–5 minutes, stirring twice. Serve hot or cold.

TWO

1. Place the oil, onion, garlic and green pepper in a bowl. Cover and microwave on HIGH for 4 minutes, stirring once.

2. Add the tomatoes, courgettes, mushrooms, thyme, tomato purée and salt and pepper to taste, blending well. Cover and microwave on HIGH for 8–10 minutes, stirring twice. Serve hot or cold.

FREEZABILITY

Ratatouille will freeze well for up to 2 months. Cook and reheat from frozen – 1 portion should be cooked on DEFROST for 5 minutes then on HIGH for 2–3 minutes, stirring twice; 2 portions should be cooked on DEFROST for 10 minutes then on HIGH for 4–5 minutes, stirring twice.

See photograph on page 82·83

FENNEL AND TOMATOES

Fennel is a delicious vegetable that tastes rather like celery but stronger. Here it is joined with tomatoes, onion, garlic and parsley to make a tasty vegetable accompaniment.

ONE		TWO
½	**fennel bulb, washed, trimmed and cut into quarters**	1
30 ml/2 tbsp	**water**	60 ml/4 tbsp
1 × 225 g/8 oz	**can peeled tomatoes, drained and coarsely chopped**	1 × 398 g/14 oz
½	**small onion, peeled and finely chopped**	1
1.25 ml/¼ tsp	**garlic purée**	2.5 ml/½ tsp
5 ml/1 tsp	**chopped fresh parsley**	10 ml/2 tsp
	salt and freshly ground black pepper	

ONE

1. Place the fennel in a dish with the water. Cover and microwave on HIGH for 2½–3 minutes.

2. Drain thoroughly and add the tomatoes, onion, garlic, parsley and salt and pepper to taste, blending well. Cover and microwave on HIGH for 5–6 minutes, stirring once.

3. Allow to stand, covered, for 5 minutes before serving.

TWO

1. Place the fennel in a dish with the water. Cover and microwave on HIGH for 5 minutes.

2. Drain thoroughly and add the tomatoes, onion, garlic, parsley and salt and pepper to taste, blending well. Cover and microwave on HIGH for 10 minutes, stirring once.

3. Allow to stand, covered, for 5 minutes before serving.

See photograph on page 82·83

Chicken livers with grapes (page 68) and Spiced chicken and mango (page 70).

OVERLEAF

From left: Ratatouille (this page) Baby onions with cream and chives (page 87), Chinese stir fry vegetables (page 86) and Fennel and tomatoes (recipe above).

MANGETOUT À LA FRANÇAISE

A variation on a classic theme, mangetout are used in this delicious vegetable accompaniment instead of the traditional petits pois.

ONE		TWO
7 g/¼ oz	**butter**	15 g/½ oz
2	**spring onions, thickly sliced**	4
100 g/4 oz	**mangetout, topped and tailed**	225 g/8 oz
60 ml/4 tbsp	**chicken stock**	120 ml/4 fl oz
2.5 ml/½ tsp	**chopped fresh mixed herbs**	5 ml/1 tsp
	pinch of salt	
2.5 ml/½ tsp	**cornflour**	5 ml/1 tsp
1	**small lettuce hearts, quartered**	2
15 ml/1 tbsp	**double cream**	30 ml/2 tbsp

ONE

1. Place the butter and spring onion in a bowl. Cover and microwave on HIGH for ½ minute.

2. Add the mangetout, chicken stock and herbs, blending well. Cover and microwave on HIGH for 1½–2 minutes, stirring once.

3. Mix the salt with the cornflour and enough water to make a smooth paste. Stir into the mangetout mixture, blending well. Cover and microwave on HIGH for ½ minute, stirring once.

4. Add the lettuce heart and cream, blending well. Cover and microwave on HIGH for ¼–½ minute until the lettuce is just cooked but not limp. Serve at once.

TWO

1. Place the butter and spring onion in a bowl. Cover and microwave on HIGH for 1 minute.

2. Add the mangetout, chicken stock and herbs, blending well. Cover and microwave on HIGH for 3–3½ minutes, stirring once.

3. Mix the salt with the cornflour and enough water to make a smooth paste. Stir into the mangetout mixture, blending well. Cover and microwave on HIGH for ¾–1 minute, stirring once.

4. Add the lettuce hearts and cream, blending well. Cover and microwave on HIGH for ½–¾ minute until the lettuce is just cooked but not limp. Serve at once.

BROCCOLI AND HAM IN CHEESE SAUCE

When you want a quick, tasty meal in a hurry this savoury vegetable dish will fit the bill. Use smoked cheese in the cheese sauce for an unusual flavour.

ONE		TWO
1	**large frozen broccoli spears**	2
1	**slices cooked ham**	2
1	**recipe hot Cheese Sauce (see page 95)**	1
15 g/½ oz	**grated cheese**	25 g/1 oz

ONE

1. Place the broccoli in a dish. Cover and microwave on HIGH for 2 minutes until cooked. Drain if necessary.

2. Roll the broccoli spear in the ham and place in a dish.

3. Pour over the sauce and sprinkle with the cheese. Microwave on HIGH for 2–2½ minutes until hot and bubbly. Serve hot.

TWO

1. Place the broccoli in a dish. Cover and microwave on HIGH for 3–4 minutes until cooked. Drain if necessary.

2. Roll the broccoli spears in the ham and place in a dish.

3. Pour over the sauce and sprinkle with the cheese. Microwave on HIGH for 4–4½ minutes until hot and bubbly. Serve hot.

Grapefruit and avocado salad (page 90) and Chilli sausage pasta salad (page 92).

CHINESE STIR FRY VEGETABLES

It is essential to use a browning dish in the preparation of this recipe because a hot surface is needed to sizzle and sear the cut vegetables.

ONE		TWO
5 ml/1 tsp	**sesame oil**	10 ml/2 tsp
¼	**small onion, peeled and sliced**	½
½	**small red pepper cored, seeded and sliced**	1
1	**small courgettes, cut into thin julienne strips**	2
1	**carrots, peeled and cut into thin julienne strips**	2
2.5 ml/½ tsp	**finely chopped fresh root ginger**	5 ml/1 tsp
25 g/1 oz	**button mushrooms wiped and sliced**	50 g/2 oz
1.25 ml/¼ tsp	**cornflour**	2.5 ml/½ tsp
7.5 ml/1½ tsp	**soy sauce**	15 ml/1 tbsp
7.5 ml/1½ tsp	**dry sherry**	15 ml/1 tbsp
	pinch of Chinese 5 spice powder	

ONE

1. Preheat a browning dish on HIGH for 8 minutes or according to the manufacturer's instructions. Add the oil and swirl to coat the base of the dish. Microwave on high for ½ minute.

2. Add the onion, pepper, courgettes, carrots and ginger, blending well. Microwave on HIGH for 2 minutes, stirring twice.

3. Add the mushrooms, blending well. Microwave on HIGH for a further ½ minute.

4. Blend the cornflour with the soy sauce, sherry and Chinese 5 spice powder. Stir into the vegetable mixture and microwave on HIGH for ½–¾ minute, stirring twice until the juices are boiling and thickened. Stir to coat the vegetables and serve at once.

TWO

1. Preheat a browning dish on HIGH for 8 minutes or according to the manufacturer's instructions. Add the oil and swirl to coat the base of the dish. Microwave on HIGH for ½ minute.

2. Add the onion, pepper, courgettes, carrots and ginger, blending well. Microwave on HIGH for 3 minutes, stirring twice.

3. Add the mushrooms, blending well. Microwave on HIGH for a further minute.

4. Blend the cornflour with the soy sauce, sherry and Chinese 5 spice powder. Stir into the vegetable mixture and microwave on HIGH for 1–1½ minutes, stirring twice until the juices are boiling and thickened. Stir to coat the vegetables and serve at once.

COOK'S TIP

When preparing Chinese stir fried vegetables for a special meal try cutting the vegetables into flower, fish, arrow, star or moon shapes using a sharp knife or small canapé cutters.

See photograph on page 82·83

LEMON GLAZED CARROTS

These strips of carrot cooked in a citrus butter are delicious served with fish, game or poultry.

ONE		TWO
100 g/4 oz	**young carrots, peeled and sliced diagonally into strips**	225 g/8 oz
30 ml/2 tbsp	**lemon juice**	60 ml/4 tbsp
7 g/¼ oz	**butter**	15 g/½ oz
1.25 ml/¼ tsp	**brown sugar**	2.5 ml/½ tsp
1.25 ml/¼ tsp	**finely grated lemon rind**	2.5 ml/½ tsp
	salt and freshly ground black pepper	
	chopped fresh parsley, to garnish	

ONE

1. Place the carrots and lemon juice in a dish. Cover and microwave on HIGH for 3–4 minutes, stirring once. Drain thoroughly.

2. Place the butter, sugar and lemon rind in a bowl and microwave on HIGH for ¼ minute.

3. Add the carrots with salt and pepper to taste and toss well to coat in the butter mixture.

4. Cover and microwave on HIGH for ¼–½ minute. Garnish with chopped parsley; serve hot.

TWO

1. Place the carrots and lemon juice in a dish. Cover and microwave on HIGH for 7–8 minutes, stirring once. Drain thoroughly.

2. Place the butter, sugar and lemon rind in a bowl and microwave on HIGH for ½ minute.

3. Add the carrots with salt and pepper to taste and toss well to coat in the butter mixture.

4. Cover and microwave on HIGH for ½–1 minute. Garnish sprinkled with chopped parsley; serve hot.

BABY ONIONS WITH CREAM AND CHIVES

Onions are one of the most versatile vegetables to combine with meat, fish and poultry but also make delicious vegetables on their own.

ONE		TWO
100 g/4 oz	**small whole baby onions, peeled**	225 g/8 oz
7.5 ml/1½ tsp	**water**	15 ml/1 tbsp
45 ml/3 tbsp	**soured cream**	75 ml/5 tbsp
10 ml/2 tsp	**milk**	20 ml/4 tsp
5 ml/1 tsp	**snipped fresh chives**	10 ml/2 tsp
	salt and freshly ground black pepper	

ONE

1. Place the onions and water in a bowl. Cover and microwave on HIGH for 2–3 minutes, stirring once. Drain thoroughly.

2. Mix the soured cream with the milk, chives and salt and pepper to taste, blending well. Pour over the onions and toss gently to coat.

3. Reduce the power setting to MEDIUM and microwave for ½ minute to reheat. Serve at once.

TWO

1. Place the onions and water in a bowl. Cover and microwave on HIGH for 4–6 minutes, stirring once. Drain thoroughly.

2. Mix the soured cream with the milk, chives and salt and pepper to taste, blending well. Pour over the onions and toss gently to coat.

3. Reduce the power setting to MEDIUM and microwave for 1 minute to reheat. Serve at once.

See photograph on page 82-83

CAULIFLOWER CHEESE

A tasty vegetable accompaniment which can also become a quick supper dish – with a little chopped cooked ham.

ONE		TWO
175 g/6 oz	**cauliflower florets**	350 g/12 oz
45 ml/3 tbsp	**water**	90 ml/6 tbsp
	pinch of salt	
150 ml/¼ pint	**hot Cheese Sauce (see page 95)**	300 ml/½ pint
15 ml/1 tbsp	**grated cheese**	30 ml/2 tbsp
	sweet paprika	

ONE

1. Place the cauliflower florets, water and a pinch of salt in a bowl. Cover and microwave on HIGH for 4–5 minutes until tender, stirring once.

2. Drain thoroughly and place in a serving dish. Spoon over the hot sauce, sprinkle with the cheese and a little paprika. Microwave on HIGH for 1 minute. Brown under a preheated grill, if liked.

TWO

1. Place the cauliflower florets, water and a pinch of salt in a bowl. Cover and microwave on HIGH for 7–8 minutes until tender, stirring once.

2. Drain thoroughly and place in a serving dish. Spoon over the hot sauce, sprinkle with cheese and paprika. Microwave on HIGH for 1½–2 minutes. Brown under a preheated grill, if liked.

POPPYSEED AND PINE NUT POTATO SALAD

A new potato salad mixed with crunchy poppyseeds and pine nuts in a light creamy dressing.

ONE		TWO
100 g/4 oz	**new potatoes, scrubbed and cut into bite-sized chunks**	225 g/8 oz
¼	**small onion, peeled and chopped**	½
15 ml/1 tbsp	**water**	30 ml/2 tbsp
15 ml/1 tbsp	**mayonnaise**	30 ml/2 tbsp
5 ml/1 tsp	**soured cream or natural yogurt**	10 ml/2 tsp
	salt and freshly ground black pepper	
15 g/½ oz	**pine nuts, toasted**	25 g/1 oz
5 ml/1 tsp	**chopped fresh parsley**	10 ml/2 tsp
2.5 ml/½ tsp	**poppyseeds**	5 ml/1 tsp

ONE

1. Place the potatoes, onion and water in a bowl. Cover and microwave on HIGH for 3 minutes, stirring once. Leave to stand for 2 minutes then drain thoroughly.

2. Mix the mayonnaise with the soured cream or yogurt and salt and pepper to taste. Stir into the potato mixture. Fold in the pine nuts and parsley, blending well.

3. Sprinkle with the poppyseeds and serve hot or cold.

TWO

1. Place the potatoes, onion and water in a bowl. Cover and microwave on HIGH for 6 minutes, stirring once. Leave to stand for 2 minutes then drain thoroughly.

2. Mix the mayonnaise with the soured cream or yogurt and salt and pepper to taste. Stir into the potato mixture. Fold in the pine nuts and parsley, blending well.

3. Sprinkle with the poppyseeds and serve hot or cold.

See photograph on page 48

CURRIED RICE, CHICKEN AND BEAN SALAD

Cooked chicken or canned blackeye beans are used in this fruity rice salad but cooked flageolet, cannellini or haricot beans could be used instead.

ONE		TWO
25 g/1 oz	**long-grain white rice**	50 g/2 oz
150 ml/¼ pint	**boiling water**	300 ml/½ pint
100 g/4 oz	**cooked or canned blackeye beans**	225 g/8 oz
15 g/½ oz	**sultanas**	25 g/1 oz
25 g/1 oz	**mushrooms, sliced**	50 g/2 oz
1	**small celery sticks, scrubbed and sliced**	2
¼	**red pepper, cored, seeded and chopped**	½
15 g/½ oz	**dried apricots, chopped**	25 g/1 oz
75 g/3 oz	**cooked chicken, skinned and chopped**	175 g/6 oz
	Dressing:	
25 ml/5 tsp	**mayonnaise**	45 ml/3 tbsp
2.5 ml/½ tsp	**curry paste**	5 ml/1 tsp
2.5 ml/½ tsp	**mango chutney**	5 ml/1 tsp
	salt and freshly ground black pepper	

ONE

1. Place the rice and water in a bowl. Cover and microwave on HIGH for 3 minutes. Reduce the power setting and microwave on MEDIUM for 12 minutes, stirring once. Leave to stand for 5 minutes. Drain if necessary and refresh under cold water.

2. Mix the rice with the beans, sultanas, mushrooms, celery, pepper, apricots and chicken, blending well.

3. To make the dressing, blend the mayonnaise with the curry paste, mango chutney and salt and pepper.

4. Add the dressing to the salad and toss well to mix.

TWO

1. Place the rice and water in a bowl. Cover and microwave on HIGH for 3 minutes. Reduce the power setting and microwave on MEDIUM for 12 minutes, stirring once. Leave to stand for 5 minutes.

Drain if necessary and refresh under cold water.

2. Mix the rice with the beans, sultanas, mushrooms, celery, pepper, apricots and chicken, blending well.

3. To make the dressing, blend the mayonnaise with the curry paste, mango chutney and salt and pepper.

4. Add the dressing to the salad and toss well to mix.

POTATO, BEAN AND DILL PICKLE SALAD

This Swedish style salad is delicious served with wafer thin slices of rare roast beef or spiced ham.

ONE		TWO
175 g/6 oz	**small new potatoes, scrubbed**	350 g/12 oz
45 ml/3 tbsp	**water**	90 ml/6 tbsp
50 g/2 oz	**cooked red kidney beans**	100 g/4 oz
¼	**small onion, peeled and chopped**	½
½	**dill pickle, finely chopped**	1
	Dressing:	
15 ml/1 tbsp	**double cream**	30 ml/2 tbsp
7.5 ml/1½ tsp	**mayonnaise**	15 ml/1 tbsp
2.5 ml/½ tsp	**Dijon mustard**	5 ml/1 tsp
	salt and freshly ground black pepper	

ONE

1. Place the potatoes and water in a bowl. Cover and microwave on HIGH for 5–6 minutes until tender. Drain then cut into bite-sized pieces. Allow to cool.

2. Mix the potatoes with the beans, onion and dill pickle.

3. To make the dressing, blend the cream with the mayonnaise, mustard and salt and pepper to taste.

4. Add the dressing to the salad and toss well to mix. Serve lightly chilled.

TWO

1. Place the potatoes and water in a bowl. Cover and microwave on HIGH for 9–10 minutes until tender. Drain then cut into bite-sized pieces. Allow to cool.

2. Mix the potatoes with the beans, onion and dill pickle.

3. To make the dressing, blend the cream with the mayonnaise, mustard and salt and pepper to taste.

4. Add the dressing to the salad and toss well to mix. Serve lightly chilled.

SPINACH AND BACON SALAD

It is essential to use only young tender spinach leaves for this salad, older leaves are too bitter.

ONE		TWO
100 g/4 oz	**young spinach leaves**	225 g/8 oz
40 g/1½ oz	**back bacon, rinded**	75 g/3 oz
½	**small green pepper, cored, seeded and sliced**	1
1	**hard-boiled eggs, shelled and quartered**	2
30 ml/2 tbsp	**French dressing**	60 ml/4 tbsp
	snipped fresh chives, to garnish	

ONE

1. Strip the spinach leaves from their stems, wash thoroughly and dry. Place in a serving bowl.

2. Place the bacon on a plate, cover with absorbent kitchen towel and microwave on HIGH for 2–3 minutes until crisp. Cool then crumble coarsely.

3. Add the bacon, pepper and hard-boiled egg to the spinach. Pour over the dressing and toss lightly to mix.

4. Garnish with snipped chives and serve at once.

TWO

1. Strip the spinach leaves from their stems, wash thoroughly and dry. Place in a serving bowl.

2. Place the bacon on a plate, cover with absorbent kitchen towel and microwave on HIGH for 3½–4½ minutes until crisp. Cool then crumble coarsely.

3. Add the bacon, pepper and hard-boiled egg to the spinach. Pour over the dressing and toss to mix.

4. Garnish with snipped chives and serve at once.

GRAPEFRUIT, RICE AND AVOCADO SALAD

Sweet and savoury rice dishes taste all the more delicious if you substitute half of the cooking water for fruit juice. In this tasty rice salad sharp grapefruit juice has been used.

ONE		TWO
50 g/2 oz	**long-grain white rice**	100 g/4 oz
150 ml/¼ pint	**boiling water**	300 ml/½ pint
150 ml/¼ pint	**unsweetened grapefruit juice**	300 ml/½ pint
½	**avocado, peeled, stoned and chopped**	1
1	**tomato, skinned, seeded and chopped**	2
25 g/1 oz	**mushrooms, wiped and sliced**	50 g/2 oz
1	**hard-boiled egg, shelled and chopped**	2
20 ml/4 tsp	**French dressing**	45 ml/3 tbsp
	salt and freshly ground black pepper	

ONE

1. Place the rice, water and grapefruit juice in a bowl. Cover and microwave on HIGH for 3 minutes. Reduce the power setting and microwave on MEDIUM for 12 minutes, stirring once. Leave to stand for 5 minutes. Drain if necessary and refresh under cold running water.

2. Mix the rice with the avocado, tomato, mushrooms and egg, blending well.

3. Pour over the dressing and add salt and pepper to taste. Toss well to blend. Serve lightly chilled.

TWO

1. Place the rice, water and grapefruit juice in a bowl. Cover and microwave on HIGH for 3 minutes. Reduce the power setting and microwave on MEDIUM for 12 minutes, stirring once. Leave to stand for 5 minutes. Drain if necessary and refresh under cold running water.

2. Mix the rice with the avocado, tomato, mushrooms and egg, blending well.

3. Pour over the dressing and add salt and pepper to taste. Toss well to blend. Serve lightly chilled.

See photograph on page 84

PEAR BEL PAESE SALAD

Pears, arranged with grapefruit and topped with a creamy cheese dressing, make an elegant salad; serve as a starter.

ONE		TWO
1	**ripe medium William or Packham pears, peeled, halved and cored**	2
25 ml/1 fl oz	**water**	50 ml/2 fl oz
1	**lemon slices**	2
	sprig of fresh tarragon	
25 g/1 oz	**Bel Paese cheese**	50 g/2 oz
15 ml/1 tbsp	**mayonnaise**	30 ml/2 tbsp
15 ml/1 tbsp	**natural yogurt**	30 ml/2 tbsp
1	**grapefruit, peeled, pith removed and sliced into segments**	2
	chopped fresh tarragon, to garnish	

ONE

1. Place the pear halves, water, lemon slice and tarragon sprig in a bowl. Cover and microwave on HIGH for 2–3 minutes or until the pear is tender. Leave to cool in the cooking liquid.

2. Meanwhile mix the cheese with the mayonnaise and yogurt, blending well. Chill thoroughly.

3. Remove the pears from the cooking liquid with a slotted spoon. Slice thickly lengthways and arrange with the grapefruit segments on a serving plate.

4. Beat the dressing to blend then spoon evenly over the salad. Garnish with chopped fresh tarragon.

TWO

1. Place the pear halves, water, lemon slices and tarragon sprig in a bowl. Cover and microwave on HIGH for 4–6 minutes or until the pears are tender. Leave to cool in the cooking liquid.

2. Meanwhile mix the cheese with the mayonnaise and yogurt, blending well. Chill thoroughly.

3. Remove the pears from the cooking liquid with a slotted spoon. Slice thickly lengthways and arrange with the grapefruit segments on a serving plate.

4. Beat the dressing to blend then spoon evenly over the salad. Garnish with chopped fresh tarragon.

TROPICAL CHICKEN SALAD

An Eastern inspired chicken salad in a light curry dressing.

ONE		TWO
1 × 100 g/4 oz	**boneless chicken breasts**	2 × 100 g/4 oz
1	**banana, peeled and sliced**	2
7.5 ml/1½ tsp	**lemon juice**	15 ml/1 tbsp
25 g/1 oz	**cashew nuts**	50 g/2 oz
15 g/½ oz	**raisins**	25 g/1 oz
25 g/1 oz	**dried apricots, cut into thin slivers**	50 g/2 oz
20 ml/4 tsp	**curry mayonnaise**	45 ml/3 tbsp
	coriander sprigs, to garnish	

ONE

1. Place the chicken on a plate. Cover and microwave on HIGH for 2–2½ minutes until tender and cooked. Leave to stand until cool then remove and discard the skin.

2. Chop the chicken into bite–sized pieces and place in a bowl. Add the banana, lemon juice, nuts, raisins and apricots and toss well to mix.

3. Fold in the curry mayonnaise, coating the chicken well. Serve lightly chilled, garnished with coriander.

TWO

1. Place the chicken on a plate. Cover and microwave on HIGH for 4–5 minutes until tender and cooked. Leave to stand until cool then remove and discard the skin.

2. Chop the chicken into bite-sized pieces and place in a bowl. Add the banana, lemon juice, nuts, raisins and apricots and toss well to mix.

3. Fold in the curry mayonnaise, coating the chicken well. Serve lightly chilled, garnished with coriander.

CHICKEN PAPAYA SALAD

This salad is deceptively hot and spicy. Serve as a main dish with corn chips or crisp crackers.

ONE		TWO
1 × 100 g/4 oz	**boneless chicken breasts**	2 × 100 g/4 oz
½	**small red pepper, cored, seeded and sliced**	1
½	**small green pepper, cored seeded and sliced**	1
½	**papaya, peeled, halved, seeded and sliced**	1
½	**small green chilli, seeded and very finely chopped**	1
30 ml/2 tbsp	**mayonnaise**	60 ml/4 tbsp
15 ml/1 tbsp	**soured cream**	30 ml/2 tbsp

ONE

1. Place the chicken on a plate. Cover and microwave on HIGH for 2–2½ minutes until tender and cooked. Leave to stand until cool then remove and discard the skin. Cut the flesh into thin strips.

2. Mix the chicken with the red pepper, green pepper and papaya.

3. Mix the chilli with the mayonnaise and soured cream.

4. Fold into the chicken mixture and chill for at least 1 hour to allow the flavours to blend. Serve lightly chilled.

TWO

1. Place the chicken on a plate. Cover and microwave on HIGH for 4–5 minutes until tender and cooked. Leave to stand until cool then remove and discard the skin. Cut the flesh into thin strips.

2. Mix the chicken with the red pepper, green pepper and papaya.

3. Mix the chilli with the mayonnaise and soured cream.

4. Fold into the chicken mixture and chill for at least 1 hour to allow the flavours to blend. Serve lightly chilled.

CHILLI SAUSAGE PASTA SALAD

A good combination of textures and flavours make this an unusual salad to serve during winter and summer.

ONE		TWO
50 g/2 oz	**dried pasta shapes**	100 g/4 oz
300 ml/½ pint	**boiling water**	450 ml/¾ pint
	salt and freshly ground black pepper	
60 g/2½ oz	**cooked red kidney beans**	150 g/5 oz
50 g/2 oz	**smoked sausage, sliced**	100 g/4 oz
¼	**small red onion, peeled and sliced**	½
25 g/1 oz	**canned sweetcorn kernels with peppers**	50 g/2 oz
15 ml/1 tbsp	**mayonnaise**	30 ml/2 tbsp
1.25 ml/¼ tsp	**chilli powder**	2.5 ml/½ tsp

ONE

1. Place the pasta in a deep bowl with the boiling water and salt to taste. Cover and microwave on HIGH for 12–14 minutes, stirring once, then allow to stand for 5–10 minutes or until tender. Drain and refresh under cold running water.
2. Mix the cold pasta with the beans, sausage, onion and sweetcorn.
3. Mix the mayonnaise with the chilli powder and salt and pepper to taste, blending well.
4. Add the dressing to the salad and toss gently.

TWO

1. Place the pasta in a deep bowl with the boiling water and salt to taste. Cover and microwave on HIGH for 12–14 minutes, stirring once, then allow to stand for 5–10 minutes or until tender. Drain and refresh under cold running water.
2. Mix the cold pasta with the beans, sausage, onion and sweetcorn.
3. Mix the mayonnaise with the chilli powder and salt and pepper to taste, blending well.
4. Add the dressing to the salad and toss gently.

See photograph on page 84

FUSILLI CORN SALAD

This is a hearty main course salad.

ONE		TWO
50 g/2 oz	**dried pasta spirals or fusilli**	100 g/4 oz
300 ml/½ pint	**boiling water**	450 ml/¾ pint
	salt and freshly ground black pepper	
½	**ripe avocado**	1
5 ml/1 tsp	**lemon juice**	10 ml/2 tsp
40 g/1½ oz	**crabmeat**	75 g/3 oz
40 g/1½ oz	**sweetcorn kernels**	75 g/3 oz
30 ml/2 tbsp	**mayonnaise**	60 ml/4 tbsp
2.5 ml/½ tsp	**grated fresh root ginger**	5 ml/1 tsp
	snipped fresh chives, to garnish	

ONE

1. Place the pasta in a deep bowl with the boiling water and salt to taste. Cover and microwave on HIGH for 12–14 minutes, stirring once, then allow to stand for 5–10 minutes or until tender.
2. Meanwhile, peel and slice the avocado and toss in the lemon juice.
3. Drain and refresh pasta under cold running water. Mix with the avocado, crabmeat and sweetcorn.
4. Mix the mayonnaise with the root ginger and salt and pepper. Add to the salad and toss gently.
5. Serve lightly chilled, garnished with chives.

TWO

1. Place the pasta in a deep bowl with the boiling water and salt to taste. Cover and microwave on HIGH for 12–14 minutes, stirring once, then allow to stand for 5–10 minutes or until tender.
2. Meanwhile, peel and slice the avocado and toss in the lemon juice.
3. Drain and refresh pasta under cold running water. Mix with the avocado, crabmeat and sweetcorn.
4. Mix the mayonnaise with the root ginger and salt and pepper, blending well. Add to the salad and toss gently.
5. Serve lightly chilled, garnished with chives.

HI-FI SALAD

The sesame seeds give an unexpected crunchy finish to this wholesome high fibre side salad.

ONE		TWO
5 ml/1 tsp	**sesame seeds**	10 ml/2 tsp
2.5 ml/½ tsp	**oil**	5 ml/1 tsp
25 g/1 oz	**brown rice**	50 g/2 oz
300 ml/½ pint	**boiling water**	450 ml/¾ pint
50 g/2 oz	**fresh or canned sweetcorn kernels**	100 g/4 oz
2	**spring onions trimmed and sliced**	4
1	**celery sticks, scrubbed and sliced**	2
15 g/½ oz	**medium carrot, grated**	25 g/1 oz
15 ml/1 tbsp	**mayonnaise**	30 ml/2 tbsp
	salt and freshly ground black pepper	

ONE

1. Place the sesame seeds and oil in a small bowl and microwave on HIGH for ½–1 minute until golden. Drain on absorbent kitchen towel.

2. Place the rice and water in a bowl. Cover and microwave on HIGH for 5 minutes. Reduce the power setting and microwave on MEDIUM for 12–15 minutes, stirring once. Leave to stand for 5–10 minutes. Drain and refresh under cold water.

3. Mix the rice with the sweetcorn, spring onions, celery, carrot, mayonnaise and salt and pepper. Serve cold sprinkled with the sesame seeds.

TWO

1. Place the sesame seeds and oil in a small bowl and microwave on HIGH for ¾–1 minute until golden. Drain on absorbent kitchen towel.

2. Place the rice and water in a bowl. Cover and microwave on HIGH for 5 minutes. Reduce the power setting and microwave on MEDIUM for 12–15 minutes, stirring once. Leave to stand for 5–10 minutes. Drain and refresh under cold water.

3. Mix the cold rice with the sweetcorn, spring onions, celery, carrot, mayonnaise and salt and pepper to taste, blending well. Serve cold sprinkled with the sesame seeds.

SAVOURY RICE

Rice makes the perfect accompaniment to many main meal dishes. However, when something a little more exciting than plain boiled rice is required – try this version.

ONE		TWO
15 g/½ oz	**butter**	25 g/1 oz
½	**small onion, peeled and chopped**	1
½	**small red pepper, cored, seeded and sliced**	1
1	**celery sticks, scrubbed and sliced**	2
25 g/1 oz	**long-grain white rice**	50 g/2 oz
150 ml/¼ pint	**boiling stock or water**	300 ml/½ pint
	salt and freshly ground black pepper	
	pinch of ground turmeric (optional)	
25 g/1 oz	**frozen peas**	50 g/2 oz

ONE

1. Place the butter, onion, red pepper and celery in a large bowl. Cover and microwave on HIGH for 3 minutes, stirring once.

2. Add the rice, boiling stock or water, salt and pepper to taste and turmeric, if used, blending well. Cover and microwave on HIGH for 3 minutes.

3. Reduce the power setting and microwave on MEDIUM for 12 minutes, stirring once.

4. Add the peas and leave to stand, covered, for 5 minutes before serving.

TWO

1. Place the butter, onion, red pepper and celery in a large bowl. Cover and microwave on HIGH for 4–5 minutes, stirring once.

2. Add the rice, boiling stock or water, salt and pepper to taste and turmeric, if used, blending well. Cover and microwave on HIGH for 3 minutes.

3. Reduce the power setting and microwave on MEDIUM for 12 minutes, stirring once.

4. Add the peas and leave to stand, covered, for 5 minutes before serving.

CREAMED COCONUT AND PINE NUT RICE

This is the perfect rice accompaniment to serve with curries.

ONE		TWO
75 g/3 oz	**long-grain white rice**	175 g/ 6 oz
250 ml/8 fl oz	**boiling water**	450 ml/¾ pint
10 ml/2 tsp	**creamed coconut**	15 ml/1 tbsp
15 g/½ oz	**toasted pine nuts**	25 g/1 oz
	salt and freshly ground black pepper	

ONE

1. Place the rice and the water in a bowl. Cover and microwave on HIGH for 3 minutes. Reduce the power setting and microwave on medium for 12 minutes. Leave to stand, covered, for 5 minutes.

2. Stir the coconut and the pine nuts and salt and pepper to taste into the rice, blending well. Cover and microwave on HIGH for 1 minute to reheat. Serve at once.

TWO

1. Place the rice and the water in a bowl. Cover and microwave on HIGH for 3 minutes. Reduce the power setting and microwave on MEDIUM for 12 minutes. Leave to stand, covered, for 5 minutes.

2. Stir the coconut and the pine nuts and salt and pepper to taste into the rice, blending well. Cover and microwave on HIGH for 1½ minutes to reheat. Serve at once.

GARLIC BREAD ROLLS

A one and two portion variation of the typical French Stick Garlic Bread.

ONE		TWO
1	**long finger-shaped crusty bread rolls**	2
1	**recipe Garlic Butter (see page 101)**	1

ONE

1. Cut the bread roll in half and spread with the garlic butter. Sandwich together again.

2. Wrap the roll in absorbent kitchen towel and microwave on HIGH for ¼–½ minute or until the butter has just melted and the bread is warm. Serve at once.

TWO

1. Cut the bread rolls in half and spread with the garlic butter. Sandwich together again.

2. Wrap the rolls in absorbent kitchen towel and microwave on HIGH for ½–1 minute or until the butter has just melted and the bread is warm. Serve at once.

CRISPY CROÛTONS

Crisp bread croûtons make a delicious topping for soups and savoury dishes or, if tossed in a little sea salt and chopped fresh herbs, a delicious snack or cocktail nibble.

ONE		TWO
25 g/1 oz	**butter**	50 g/2 oz
1½	**large slices of bread, crusts removed and cut into small cubes**	3

ONE

1. Place the butter in a bowl and microwave on HIGH for ¾ minute to melt.

2. Add the bread cubes and toss to coat, microwave on HIGH for ¾–1 minute. Stir well and microwave on HIGH for a further ¾ minute until golden and crisp. Drain on absorbent kitchen towel.

TWO

1. Place the butter in a bowl and microwave on HIGH for 1 minute to melt.

2. Add the bread cubes and toss to coat, microwave on HIGH for 1½ minutes. Stir well and microwave on HIGH for a further 1½ minutes until golden and crisp. Drain on an absorbent kitchen towel.

Sauces, Butters, Stuffings & Dressings

BASIC WHITE POURING SAUCE

ONE		TWO
5 g/½ oz	**butter**	25 g/1 oz
15 g/½ oz	**plain flour**	25 g/1 oz
150 ml/¼ pint	**milk**	300 ml/½ pint
	salt and freshly ground black pepper	

ONE

1. Place the butter in a jug and microwave on HIGH for ¼–½ minute to melt.

2. Add the flour, blending well. Gradually add the milk and salt and pepper to taste.

3. Microwave on HIGH for 1½–2 minutes, stirring 3 times until smooth and thickened. Use as required.

TWO

1. Place the butter in a jug and microwave on HIGH for ½ minute to melt.

2. Add the flour, blending well. Gradually add the milk and salt and pepper to taste.

3. Microwave on HIGH for 3½–4 minutes, stirring 3 times until smooth and thickened. Use as required.

VARIATIONS

BASIC WHITE COATING SAUCE

Prepare and cook as above but double the quantities of both butter and flour in each case.

CHEESE SAUCE

Prepare and cook as above then add 25 g/1 oz grated cheese and a pinch of mustard powder for every 150 ml/¼ pint milk used. Stir well to blend.

PARSLEY SAUCE

Prepare and cook as above then add 7.5 ml/1½ teaspoons chopped fresh parsley for every 150 ml/¼ pint milk used. Stir well to blend.

CAPER SAUCE

Prepare and cook as above then add 1½ teaspoons chopped capers and 1 teaspoon white wine vinegar for every 150 ml/¼ pint milk used. Stir well to blend.

BÉCHAMEL SAUCE

This rich, creamy sauce cooks quickly in the microwave and emerges velvety-smooth and lump free.

ONE		TWO
1	**small onion, peeled**	1
6	**cloves**	6
1	**bay leaf**	1
3	**peppercorns**	6
½	**small carrot, peeled**	1
150 ml/¼ pint	**milk**	300 ml/½ pint
15 g/½ oz	**butter**	25 g/1 oz
15 g/½ oz	**flour**	25 g/1 oz
	salt and freshly ground black pepper	

ONE

1. Stud the onion with the cloves and place in a bowl with the bay leaf, peppercorns, carrot and milk. Cover and microwave on DEFROST power for 5–6 minutes until hot.

2. Place the butter in a jug and microwave on HIGH for ½ minute to melt. Stir in the flour, blending well. Gradually add the strained milk and salt and pepper to taste.

3. Microwave on HIGH for 1–1¼ minutes until smooth and thickened, stirring twice. Use as required.

TWO

1. Stud the onion with the cloves and place in a bowl with the bay leaf, peppercorns, carrot and milk. Cover and microwave on DEFROST power for 10–11 minutes until hot.

2. Place the butter in a jug and microwave on HIGH for ¾ minute to melt. Stir in the flour, blending well. Gradually add the strained milk and salt and pepper to taste.

3. Microwave on HIGH for 1½–2 minutes until smooth and thickened, stirring twice. Use as required.

VARIATIONS

AURORE SAUCE

Prepare and cook as above then add 15 ml/1 tbsp tomato purée and a pinch of caster sugar for every 150 ml/¼ pint milk used. Stir well to blend.

TARRAGON SAUCE

Prepare and cook as above then add 7.5 ml/1½ tsp chopped fresh tarragon for every 150 ml/¼ pint milk used. Stir well to blend.

MORNAY SAUCE

Prepare and cook as above then add 15 g/½ oz each of grated Cheddar and Parmesan cheese and a little French mustard for every 150 ml/¼ pint milk used. Whisk until the cheese melts and the sauce is smooth.

EGG AND CHIVE SAUCE

Prepare and cook as above then add 1 small chopped hard-boiled egg and 5 ml/1 tsp snipped chives for every 150 ml/¼ pint milk used. Stir well to blend.

BÉARNAISE SAUCE

It is essential to use a blender or food processor for this sauce. Serve with steaks, poached eggs on toast or cooked green vegetables.

ONE		TWO
2	**small egg yolks (size 5 or 6)**	4
3.75 ml/¾ tsp	**white wine vinegar**	7.5 ml/1½ tsp
3.75 ml/¾ tsp	**dry white wine**	7.5 ml/1½ tsp
	pinch chopped fresh or dried tarragon	
	salt and freshly ground black pepper	
40 g/1½ oz	**butter**	75 g/3 oz
7.5 ml/1½ tsp	**very finely chopped onion**	15 ml/1 tbsp

ONE

1. Place the egg yolks, wine vinegar, wine, tarragon and salt and pepper to taste in a blender. Process for about 3–5 seconds until smooth and blended.

2. Place the butter and onion in a bowl. Cover and microwave on HIGH for ½–¾ minute until hot and bubbly.

3. With the blender running on low speed, add the butter mixture to the egg yolk mixture in a steady stream until the sauce thickens.

4. Pour into a serving bowl and microwave on MEDIUM for ½–1 minute until hot, thick and creamy, stirring three times. Serve at once.

TWO

1. Place the egg yolks, wine vinegar, wine, tarragon and salt and pepper to taste in a blender. Process for about 3–5 seconds until smooth and blended.

2. Place the butter and onion in a bowl. Cover and microwave on HIGH for ¾–1¼ minutes until hot and bubbly.

3. With the blender running on a low speed, add the butter mixture to the egg yolk mixture in a steady stream until the sauce thickens.

4. Pour into a serving bowl and microwave on MEDIUM for 1–2 minutes until hot, thick and creamy, stirring three times. Serve at once.

HOLLANDAISE SAUCE

A velvety smooth sauce to serve hot with poached salmon, globe artichokes or cooked vegetables.

ONE		TWO
1	**small egg yolks (size 5 or 6)**	2
7.5 ml/1½ tsp	**lemon juice**	15 ml/1 tbsp
	salt and freshly ground white pepper	
25 g/1 oz	**butter**	50 g/2 oz

ONE

1. Place the egg yolk, lemon juice and salt and pepper to taste in a blender or small bowl and blend or whisk with a hand-held beater until frothy.

2. Dice the butter and place in a jug. Cover and microwave on HIGH for ¾ minute to melt.

3. Whisking vigorously or with the blender on high speed, slowly pour the butter into the egg mixture, blending or whisking until the sauce is very thick, smooth and creamy.

4. Return to the jug and place in a bowl of hand-hot water (making sure the water level in the bowl is the same as the sauce level).

5. Microwave, uncovered, on LOW for 1½–1¾ minutes, stirring twice. Stir and serve at once.

TWO

1. Place the egg yolk, lemon juice and salt and pepper to taste in a blender or small bowl and blend or whisk with a hand-held beater until frothy.

2. Dice the butter and place in a jug. Cover and microwave on HIGH for 1–1¼ minutes to melt.

3. Whisking vigorously or with the blender on high speed, slowly pour the butter into the egg mixture, blending or whisking until the sauce is very thick, smooth and creamy.

4. Return to the jug and place in a bowl of hand-hot water (making sure the water level in the bowl is the same as the sauce level).

5. Microwave, uncovered, on LOW for 3–3½ minutes, stirring twice. Stir and serve at once.

SWEET AND SOUR SAUCE

A must for chicken, pork and prawn sweet and sour dishes.

ONE		TWO
20 ml/4 tsp	**vinegar**	45 ml/3 tbsp
15 ml/1 tbsp	**sugar**	30 ml/2 tbsp
15 ml/1 tbsp	**cornflour**	30 ml/2 tbsp
15 ml/1 tbsp	**tomato purée**	30 ml/2 tbsp
5 ml/1 tsp	**soy sauce**	10 ml/2 tsp
½ × 225 g/8 oz	**can pineapple pieces in natural juice**	1 × 225 g/8 oz
	small piece of cucumber, cut into thin julienne strips	

ONE

1. Place the vinegar, sugar, cornflour, tomato purée, soy sauce and pineapple juice in a bowl, blending well.
2. Microwave on HIGH for 1½ minutes, stirring twice until smooth and thickened.
3. Add the pineapple pieces and cucumber, blending well. Microwave on HIGH for a further 1½–2 minutes, stirring once. Use as required.

TWO

1. Place the vinegar, sugar, cornflour, tomato purée, soy sauce and pineapple juice in a bowl, blending well.
2. Microwave on HIGH for 3 minutes, stirring twice until smooth and thickened.
3. Add the pineapple pieces and cucumber, blending well. Microwave on HIGH for a further 3 minutes, stirring once. Use as required.

SOURED CREAM MUSHROOM SAUCE

This tangy sauce is perfect for serving with pork chops, veal escalopes, gammon, chicken or game birds.

ONE		TWO
15 g/½ oz	**butter**	25 g/1 oz
50 g/2 oz	**button mushrooms, wiped and sliced**	100 g/4 oz
20 g/¾ oz	**flour**	40 g/1½ oz
30 ml/2 tbsp	**dry sherry**	60 ml/4 tbsp
75 ml/5 tbsp	**soured cream**	150 ml/¼ pint
75 ml/5 tbsp	**meat stock or cooked meat juices**	150 ml/¼ pint
	salt and freshly ground black pepper	

ONE

1. Place the butter and mushrooms in a bowl. Cover and microwave on HIGH for 1½-2 minutes, stirring once.
2. Add the flour, blending well. Microwave on HIGH for ¼ minute.
3. Gradually add the sherry, soured cream, stock or meat juices and salt and pepper to taste, blending well.
4. Reduce the power setting to MEDIUM and microwave for 4–5 minutes, stirring twice until creamy and thickened but do not allow to boil. Serve at once.

TWO

1. Place the butter and mushrooms in a bowl. Cover and microwave on HIGH for 3½ minutes, stirring once.
2. Add the flour, blending well. Microwave on HIGH for ½ minute.
3. Gradually add the sherry, soured cream, stock or meat juices and salt and pepper to taste, blending well.
4. Reduce the power setting to MEDIUM and microwave for 8 minutes, stirring twice until creamy and thickened but do not allow to boil. Serve at once.

BARBECUE SAUCE

To baste, coat or serve with plain cooked meats, fish and poultry, this sauce has just as good a flavour as more complicated long-simmered versions.

ONE		TWO
½	**small onion, peeled and chopped**	1
½	**small garlic clove, peeled and crushed**	1
75 ml/5 tbsp	**tomato ketchup**	150 ml/¼ pint
7.5 ml/1½ tsp	**water**	15 ml/1 tbsp
10 ml/2 tsp	**red wine vinegar**	20 ml/4 tsp
7.5 ml/1½ tsp	**Worcestershire sauce**	15 ml/1 tbsp
2.5 ml/½ tsp	**soy sauce**	5 ml/1 tsp
15 g/½ oz	**brown sugar**	25 g/1 oz
7.5 ml/1½ tsp	**oil**	15 ml/1 tbsp
2.5 ml/½ tsp	**lemon juice**	5 ml/1 tsp

ONE

1. Place the onion, garlic, tomato ketchup, water, vinegar, Worcestershire sauce, soy sauce, sugar, oil and lemon juice in a bowl, blending well.

2. Cover and microwave on HIGH for 2–3 minutes, stirring twice.

3. Leave to stand for 5 minutes. Use as required.

TWO

1. Place the onion, garlic, tomato ketchup, water, vinegar, Worcestershire sauce, soy sauce, sugar, oil and lemon juice in a bowl, blending well.

2. Cover and microwave on HIGH for 4–4½ minutes, stirring twice.

3. Leave to stand for 5 minutes. Use as required.

TOMATO SAUCE

This vibrant tomato sauce is equally good with pasta, hamburgers or chicken. If a chunky sauce is preferred then do not purée.

ONE		TWO
7 g/¼ oz	**butter**	15 g/½ oz
¼	**small onion, peeled and chopped**	½
7 g/¼ oz	**flour**	15 g/½ oz
100 g/4 oz	**tomatoes, skinned, seeded and chopped**	225 g/8 oz
	pinch of dried basil	
	pinch of dried oregano	
45 ml/3 tbsp	**dry red wine**	75 ml/5 tbsp
7.5 ml/1½ tsp	**tomato purée**	15 ml/1 tbsp
5 ml/1 tsp	**chopped fresh parsley**	10 ml/2 tsp
	salt and freshly ground black pepper	

ONE

1. Place the butter and onion in a bowl. Cover and microwave on HIGH for ¾ minute until soft.

2. Stir in the flour, blending well. Microwave on HIGH for a further ¼ minute.

3. Gradually add the tomatoes, basil, oregano, wine, tomato purée, parsley and salt and pepper to taste, blending well.

4. Microwave on HIGH for 2 minutes, stirring once.

5. Purée in a blender or push through a fine sieve.

TWO

1. Place the butter and onion in a bowl. Cover and microwave on HIGH for 1½ minutes until soft.

2. Stir in the flour, blending well. Microwave on HIGH for a further ¼ minute.

3. Gradually add the tomatoes, basil, oregano, wine, tomato purée, parsley and salt and pepper to taste, blending well.

4. Microwave on HIGH for 3½–4 minutes, stirring once.

5. Purée in a blender or push through a fine sieve.

GRAVY

This is a simple gravy suitable to serve with roast meats. Use the appropriate meat stock and for extra flavour try adding a little cooked onion or a few chopped fresh herbs.

ONE		TWO
7.5 ml/1½ tsp	**cooked meat pan juices or drippings**	15 ml/1 tbsp
5–7.5 ml/1–1½ tsp	**flour**	10–15 ml/2–3 tsp
75 ml/5 tbsp	**hot stock**	150 ml/¼ pint
	salt and freshly ground black pepper	

ONE

1. Place the pan juices or drippings in a bowl with the flour, blending well. Microwave on HIGH for 1–1½ minutes until the flour turns golden.
2. Gradually add the stock, blending well. Microwave on HIGH for ¾–1 minute, stirring twice until smooth and thickened. Season to taste with salt and pepper. Serve hot.

TWO

1. Place the pan juices or drippings in a bowl with the flour, blending well. Microwave on HIGH for 1½–2 minutes until the flour turns golden.
2. Gradually add the stock, blending well. Microwave on HIGH for 1½–1¾ minutes, stirring twice until smooth and boiling. Season to taste with salt and pepper. Serve hot.

GOOSEBERRY SAUCE

Deliciously sharp gooseberry sauce makes the perfect accompaniment for oily fish like mackerel, herring or trout. For a sweet sauce to serve with steamed sponge puddings, pancakes or ice cream simply increase the sugar.

ONE		TWO
225 g/8 oz	**gooseberries, topped and tailed**	450 g/1 lb
15 g/½ oz	**caster sugar**	25 g/1 oz
15 ml/1 tbsp	**water**	30 ml/2 tbsp
15 g/½ oz	**butter**	25 g/1 oz

ONE

1. Place the gooseberries in a shallow dish and sprinkle with the sugar. This quantity makes a sharp sauce to serve with fish – for a sweet sauce increase the sugar quantity to 40 g/1½ oz.
2. Add the water, cover and microwave on HIGH for 4–5 minutes until tender and soft, stirring twice.
3. Add the butter and stir to melt.
4. Purée in a blender or push through a fine sieve. Serve warm or cold.

TWO

1. Place the gooseberries in a shallow dish and sprinkle with the sugar. This quantity makes a sharp sauce to serve with fish – for a sweet sauce increase the sugar quantity to 75 g/3 oz.
2. Add the water, cover and microwave on HIGH for 8–9 minutes until tender and soft, stirring twice.
3. Add the butter and stir to melt.
4. Purée in a blender or push through a fine sieve. Serve warm or cold.

See photograph on page 45

SPEEDY CUSTARD SAUCE

Not the 'real' egg custard sauce but just as delicious.

ONE		TWO
7.5 ml/1½ tsp	**custard powder**	15 ml/ tbsp
7.5–15 ml/1½–3 tsp	**sugar**	15–30 ml/1–2 tbsp
150 ml/¼ pint	**milk**	300 ml/½ pint
	few drops of vanilla essence	

ONE

1. Mix the custard powder with the sugar and a little of the milk to make a smooth paste. Gradually blend in the remaining milk. Microwave on HIGH for 2–3 minutes until smooth and thick, whisking every 1 minute.

2. Add a few drops of vanilla essence, blending well.

TWO

1. Mix the custard powder with the sugar and a little of the milk to make a smooth paste. Gradually blend in the remaining milk. Microwave on HIGH for 3–4 minutes until smooth and thick, whisking every 1 minute.

2. Add a few drops of vanilla essence, blending well.

APPLE SAUCE

Apple sauce is an indispensable accompaniment to roast pork, but it is also tasty with sausages and game. The commercially prepared kind is never quite like the real thing so it is well worth the effort.

ONE		TWO
100 g/4 oz	**cooking apples, peeled, cored and sliced**	225 g/8 oz
	knob of butter	
	dash of lemon juice	
2.5 ml/½ tsp	**sugar**	5 ml/1 tsp
5 ml/1 tsp	**water**	10 ml/2 tsp

ONE

1. Place the apples, butter, lemon juice, sugar and water in a bowl. Cover and microwave on HIGH for 2–3 minutes until the apple is soft and tender.

2. Beat with a wooden spoon until smooth.

TWO

1. Place the apples, butter, lemon juice, sugar and water in a bowl. Cover and microwave on HIGH for 4–5 minutes until the apple is soft and tender.

2. Beat with a wooden spoon until smooth.

GARLIC BUTTER

Addicts to this butter find it irresistible with French bread, on succulent steaks, with vegetables, seafood and sandwiches. Wrap any unused garlic butter and store in the refrigerator for up to 1 week.

ONE		TWO
25 g/ oz	**butter**	50 g/2 oz
½	**garlic clove, peeled and crushed**	1
	dash of Dijon mustard	
	salt and freshly ground black pepper	

ONE

1. Place the butter in a bowl and microwave on HIGH for 5–10 seconds to soften.

2. Add the garlic, mustard and salt and pepper to taste and beat until smooth and blended. Cover and chill until required.

TWO

1. Place the butter in a bowl and microwave on HIGH for 10–15 seconds to soften.

2. Add the garlic, mustard and salt and pepper to taste and beat until smooth and blended. Cover and chill until required.

DEVILLED CHILLI BUTTER

Hot and spicy, ideal with shellfish, pork and mackerel.

ONE		TWO
25 g/1 oz	**butter**	50 g/2 oz
10 ml/2 tsp	**finely chopped red pepper**	15 ml/1 tbsp
1.25 ml/¼ tsp	**mustard powder**	2.5 ml/½ tsp
2.5 ml/½ tsp	**Worcestershire sauce**	5 ml/1 tsp
2.5 ml/½ tsp	**lemon juice**	5 ml/1 tsp
	salt and cayenne pepper	

ONE

1. Place the butter in a bowl and microwave for 5–10 seconds to soften.

2. Add the red pepper, mustard powder, Worcestershire sauce, lemon juice and salt and cayenne pepper to taste and beat until smooth and blended. Cover and chill until required.

TWO

1. Place the butter in a bowl and microwave on HIGH for 10–15 seconds to soften.

2. Add the red pepper, mustard powder, Worcestershire sauce, lemon juice and salt and cayenne pepper to taste and beat until smooth and blended. Cover and chill until required.

BLUE CHEESE AND CHIVE BUTTER

This rich creamy butter is tasty on steaks, mushrooms, sandwiches and canapés.

ONE		TWO
25 g/1 oz	**butter**	50 g/2 oz
15 g/½ oz	**blue Stilton or Danish Blue, mashed**	25 g/1 oz
10 ml/2 tsp	**snipped chives**	20 ml/4 tsp
	salt and freshly ground black pepper	

ONE

1. Place the butter in a bowl and microwave on HIGH for 5–10 seconds to soften.

2. Add the cheese, chives and salt and pepper to taste and beat until smooth and blended. Cover and chill until required.

TWO

1. Place the butter in a bowl and microwave on HIGH for 10–15 seconds to soften.

2. Add the cheese, chives and salt and pepper to taste and beat until smooth and blended. Cover and chill until required.

FESTIVE STUFFING BALLS

These tasty stuffing balls are delicious served with plain cooked chicken, turkey or pork. Cook in a microwave bun tray if available to keep a good even shape.

ONE		TWO
100 g/4 oz	**pork sausagemeat**	225 g/8 oz
25 g/1 oz	**cooked ham, finely chopped**	50 g/2 oz
½	**small onion, peeled and chopped**	1
½	**small apple, peeled, cored and grated**	1
	pinch of dried mixed herbs	
15 ml/1 tbsp	**fresh white breadcrumbs**	30 ml/2 tbsp
	salt and freshly ground black pepper	

ONE

1. Mix the sausagemeat with the ham, onion, apple, herbs, breadcrumbs and salt and pepper to taste, blending well.

2. Shape into 3 even-sized stuffing balls.

3. Arrange in a circle on a plate or in a microwave bun tray and microwave on HIGH for 5 minutes until cooked. Serve hot or cold.

TWO

1. Mix the sausagemeat with the ham, onion, apple,

herbs, breadcrumbs and salt and pepper to taste, blending well.

2. Divide and shape into 6 even-sized stuffing balls.

3. Arrange in a circle on a plate or in a microwave bun tray and microwave on HIGH for 8–10 minutes until cooked. Serve hot or cold.

HAM OAT STUFFING

A succulent mixture ideal for stuffing chicken, turkey, duck or game birds prior to roasting.

ONE		TWO
7 g/¼ oz	**butter**	15 g/½ oz
½	**small onion, peeled and grated**	1
1	**celery sticks, scrubbed and chopped**	2
15 g/½ oz	**porridge oats**	25 g/1 oz
25 g/1 oz	**fresh breadcrumbs**	50 g/2 oz
40 g/1½ oz	**cooked ham, finely chopped**	75 g/3 oz
7.5 ml/1½ tsp	**chopped fresh parsley**	15 ml/1 tbsp
½	**egg, beaten**	1
	salt and freshly ground black pepper	

ONE

1. Place the butter, onion and celery in a bowl. Microwave on HIGH for 1½–2 minutes until tender, stirring once. Allow to cool.

2. Add the oats, breadcrumbs, ham, parsley, beaten egg and salt and pepper to taste. Bind together to make a stuffing. Use as required.

TWO

1. Place the butter, onion and celery in a bowl. Microwave on HIGH for 2–3 minutes until tender, stirring once. Allow to cool.

2. Add the oats, breadcrumbs, ham, parsley, beaten egg and salt and pepper to taste. Bind together to make a stuffing. Use as required.

SAVOURY APPLE AND APRICOT STUFFING

A rich fruity stuffing ideal for pork, chicken or duck.

ONE		TWO
1 × 1 cm/½ inch	**slices white bread from a large uncut loaf, crusts removed**	2 × 1 cm/½ inch
50 ml/2 fl oz	**stock or milk**	100 ml/4 fl oz
7 g/¼ oz	**butter**	15 g/½ oz
½	**small celery stick, scrubbed and chopped**	1
15 g/½ oz	**dried apricots, coarsely chopped**	25 g/1 oz
100 g/4 oz	**cooking apples, peeled, cored and chopped**	225 g/8 oz
15 g/½ oz	**raisins**	25 g/1 oz
	pinch dried marjoram or thyme	
10 ml/2 tsp	**chopped fresh parsley**	20 ml/4 tsp
	salt and freshly ground black pepper	

ONE

1. Place the bread in a bowl with the stock or milk and leave to soak for 5 minutes.

2. Place the butter and celery in a bowl. Microwave on HIGH for 1 minute. Squeeze the bread to remove any excess stock or milk and add to the bowl with the apples, raisins, marjoram or thyme, parsley and salt and pepper to taste, blending well.

3. Use to stuff a piece of meat or shape into 3 or 4 stuffing balls. To cook separately, arrange in a ring on a plate and microwave on HIGH for 2–3 minutes. Serve hot or cold.

TWO

1. Place the bread in a bowl with the stock or milk and leave to soak for 5 minutes.

2. Place the butter and celery in a bowl. Microwave on HIGH for 1½–2 minutes. Squeeze the bread to remove any excess stock or milk and place in a bowl with the rest of the ingredients, blending well.

3. Use to stuff a piece of meat or shape into 6 or 8 stuffing balls. To cook separately, arrange in a ring on a plate and microwave on HIGH for 3–3½ minutes. Serve hot or cold.

FLORIMON DRESSING

It is essential to cook the garlic in this dressing to extract the full flavour. Use in salads or with cooked vegetables.

ONE		TWO
½	**garlic clove, halved**	1
15 ml/1 tbsp	**olive or safflower oil**	30 ml/2 tbsp
15 ml/1 tbsp	**lemon juice**	30 ml/2 tbsp
	pinch of ground paprika	
	salt	
	pinch of sugar	

ONE

1. Place the garlic and oil in a bowl. Cover and microwave on HIGH for ½ minute. Leave to stand for 5 minutes.

2. Remove the garlic with a slotted spoon and discard.

3. Gradually beat the lemon juice into the oil to make a thick creamy vinaigrette.

4. Add the paprika and salt and sugar to taste, blending well. Use at once.

TWO

1. Place the garlic and oil in a bowl. Cover and microwave on HIGH for 1 minute. Leave to stand for 5 minutes.

2. Remove the garlic with a slotted spoon and discard.

3. Gradually beat the lemon juice into the oil to make a thick creamy vinaigrette.

4. Add the paprika and salt and sugar to taste, blending well. Use at once.

MOCK MAYONNAISE

A cooked mayonnaise-style dressing thickened with set natural yogurt.

ONE		TWO
5 ml/1 tsp	**plain flour**	10 ml/2 tsp
2.5 ml/½ tsp	**mustard powder**	5 ml/1 tsp
20 ml/4 tsp	**brown sugar**	40 ml/8 tsp
50 ml/2 fl oz	**water**	100 ml/4 fl oz
½	**egg yolk**	1
10 ml/2 tsp	**wine vinegar**	20 ml/4 tsp
50 ml/2 fl oz	**olive or safflower oil**	100 ml/4 fl oz
	salt and freshly ground black pepper	
10 ml/2 tsp	**snipped chives (optional)**	20 ml/4 tsp
15–30 ml/1–2 tbsp	**set natural yogurt**	30–60 ml/2–4 tbsp

ONE

1. Mix the flour with the mustard, sugar and water in a bowl, blending well. Microwave on HIGH for 2–2½ minutes, stirring three times.

2. Meanwhile mix the egg yolk with the vinegar and oil, blending well. Add the mustard mixture and whisk well to blend.

3. Add salt and pepper to taste and chives if liked, blending well. Allow to cool.

4. Stir the yogurt into the cold dressing just before serving.

TWO

1. Mix the flour with the mustard, sugar and water in a bowl, blending well. Microwave on HIGH for 4 minutes, stirring three times.

2. Meanwhile mix the egg yolks with the vinegar and oil, blending well. Add the mustard mixture and whisk well to blend.

3. Add salt and pepper to taste and chives if liked, blending well. Allow to cool.

4. Stir the yogurt into the cold dressing just before serving.

Desserts

GLAZED ORANGES

This is an ideal way of serving the juicy summer oranges that are cheap and plentiful from May to October. Serve with an unusual ice cream for a special occasion – almond complements their flavour admirably.

ONE		TWO
2	**small summer oranges**	4
45 ml/3 tbsp	**water**	90 ml/6 tbsp
75 g/3 oz	**granulated sugar**	175 g/6 oz

ONE

1. Peel the oranges, removing the pith and membrane, slice thinly and put into a serving dish.

2. Place the water and sugar in a bowl. Microwave on HIGH for 2–3 minutes until bubbly and syrupy, stirring 3 times.

3. Pour the syrup over the oranges and leave until cold. Chill thoroughly before serving.

TWO

1. Peel the oranges, removing the pith and membrane, slice thinly and put into a serving dish.

2. Place the water and sugar in a bowl. Microwave on HIGH for 4–5 minutes until bubbly and syrupy, stirring 3 times.

3. Pour the syrup over the oranges and leave until cold. Chill thoroughly before serving.

COOK'S TIP

Try using fruit such as peaches, nectarines or grapes instead of oranges.

FRUIT TRIFLE

More indulgent than a fresh fruit salad, a fresh fruit trifle with its creamy custard topping and sherried fruit and sponge base, is just as quick and easy to make from scratch.

ONE		TWO
1	**slices stale sponge cake**	2
10 ml/2 tsp	**jam**	20 ml/4 tsp
150 g/5 oz	**fresh fruit salad**	275 g/10 oz
10 ml/2 tsp	**sherry**	20 ml/4 tsp
7.5 ml/1½ tsp	**custard powder**	15 ml/1 tbsp
7.5–15 ml/1½–3 tsp	**sugar**	15–30 ml/1–2 tbsp
150 ml/¼ pint	**milk**	300 ml/½ pint
	few drops of vanilla essence	
	whipped cream, to decorate	

ONE

1. Spread the sponge cake with the jam, cut into cubes and place in a serving dish.
2. Spoon over the fruit salad and sherry.
3. Mix the custard powder with sugar to taste and a little of the milk to make a smooth paste.
4. Gradually blend in the remaining milk and microwave on HIGH for 2–3 minutes until smooth and thick, whisking every minute.
5. Add a few drops of vanilla essence to taste, blending well. Leave to cool slightly then pour over the fruit and sponge mixture. Chill until set.
6. Serve lightly chilled, decorated with swirls of whipped cream.

TWO

1. Spread the sponge cake with the jam, cut into cubes and place in a serving dish.
2. Spoon over the fruit salad and sherry.
3. Mix the custard powder with sugar to taste and a little of the milk to make a smooth paste.
4. Gradually blend in the remaining milk and microwave on HIGH for 3–4 minutes until smooth and thick, whisking every minute.
5. Add a few drops of vanilla essence to taste, blending well. Leave to cool slightly then pour over the fruit and sponge mixture. Chill until set.
6. Serve lightly chilled, decorated with swirls of whipped cream.

RED FRUITS SALAD

Fruit salads are naturally colourful and very easy to make. Use grenadine fruit syrup as the base for this delicious summer dessert.

ONE		TWO
25 g/1 oz	**blackcurrants, topped and tailed**	50 g/2 oz
20 ml/4 tsp	**grenadine fruit syrup**	40 ml/8 tsp
20 ml/4 tsp	**water**	40 ml/8 tsp
25 g/1 oz	**raspberries, hulled**	50 g/2 oz
25 g/1 oz	**strawberries, hulled and sliced**	50 g/2 oz
25 g/1 oz	**cherries, halved and stoned**	50 g/2 oz

ONE

1. Place the blackcurrants, grenadine fruit syrup and water in a bowl. Cover and microwave on HIGH for 1 minute stirring once.
2. Transfer to a serving bowl and stir in the raspberries, strawberries and cherries, blending well.
3. Chill thoroughly before serving with single cream.

TWO

1. Place the blackcurrants, grenadine fruit syrup and water in a bowl. Cover and microwave on HIGH for 1½ minutes stirring once.
2. Transfer to a serving bowl and stir in the raspberries, strawberries and cherries, blending well.
3. Chill thoroughly before serving with single cream.

COOK'S TIP

Try using red wine instead of the water, redcurrants instead of the blackcurrants and blackcurrant syrup instead of the grenadine syrup.

See photograph on page 117

MULLED FRUITS WITH PORT

A delicious mixture of berry fruits and melon nestling in a port wine syrup. Use sherry as an alternative to port if preferred.

ONE		TWO
7.5 ml/1½ tsp	**orange or lemon juice**	15 ml/1 tbsp
25 ml/1 fl oz	**port**	50 ml/2 fl oz
	pinch of ground nutmeg	
	pinch of ground mixed spice	
2	**cloves**	2
7 g/¼ oz	**caster sugar**	15 g/½ oz
50 g/2 oz	**strawberries, hulled, left whole or sliced**	100 g/4 oz
50 g/2 oz	**raspberries**	100 g/4 oz
50 g/2 oz	**melon, diced**	100 g/4 oz
	mint sprigs, to decorate (optional)	

ONE

1. Place the orange or lemon juice, port, nutmeg, mixed spice, cloves and sugar in a bowl. Microwave on HIGH for 1 minute, stirring twice. Remove and discard the cloves.

2. Place the strawberries, raspberries and melon in a serving bowl. Pour over the port syrup. Serve hot or cold decorated with mint sprigs.

TWO

1. Place the orange or lemon juice, port, nutmeg, mixed spice, cloves and sugar in a bowl. Microwave on HIGH for 2 minutes, stirring twice. Remove and discard the cloves.

2. Place the strawberries, raspberries and melon in a bowl. Pour over the port syrup. Serve hot or cold decorated with mint sprigs.

PINEAPPLE PROMISE

One of the simplest creamy but refreshing chilled summer desserts I know. Serve on the day of making.

ONE		TWO
¼ × 375 g/13 oz	**can crushed pineapple**	½ × 375 g/13 oz
3.75 ml/¾ tsp	**powdered gelatine**	7.5 ml/1½ tsp
45 ml/3 tbsp	**double cream**	75 ml/5 tbsp
150 ml/¼ pint	**cold Speedy Custard Sauce (see page 100)**	300 ml/½ pint
	whipped cream and pistachio nuts, to decorate	

ONE

1. Drain the syrup from the crushed pineapple and mix with the gelatine. Leave for about 5 minutes until spongy then microwave on HIGH for ¼–½ minute until clear and dissolved.

2. Whip the cream until it stands in soft peaks and fold into the pineapple with the custard and the gelatine mixture. Spoon into a dessert glass and chill until set.

3. Decorate with swirls of whipped cream and pistachio nuts and serve with crisp dessert biscuits.

TWO

1. Drain the syrup from the crushed pineapple and mix with the gelatine. Leave for about 5 minutes until spongy then microwave on HIGH for ½ minute until clear and dissolved.

2. Whip the cream until it stands in soft peaks and fold into the pineapple with the custard and the gelatine mixture. Spoon into dessert glasses and chill until set.

3. Decorate with swirls of whipped cream and pistachio nuts and serve with crisp dessert biscuits.

COOK'S TIP

Substitute other favourite canned fruit for the pineapple, if preferred.

PEARS BELLE HÉLÈNE

My variation of the classic pear and chocolate sauce dessert.

ONE		TWO
1	**trifle sponges**	2
15 ml/1 tbsp	**chocolate and hazelnut spread**	30 ml/2 tbsp
1	**canned pear halves, drained**	2
1	**small scoops vanilla ice cream**	2
25 g/1 oz	**plain chocolate**	50 g/2 oz
15 g/½ oz	**butter**	25 g/1 oz
15 ml/1 tbsp	**milk**	30 ml/2 tbsp
	whipped cream and chocolate leaves, to decorate	

ONE

1. Using a sharp knife, halve the trifle sponge horizontally and sandwich together with the chocolate and hazelnut spread. Place in a serving dish.

2. Put the ice cream into the pear hollow and place ice cream side down on the trifle sponge. Keep cool.

3. Place the chocolate in a bowl with the butter. Microwave on HIGH for 1–1¼ minutes to melt. Add the milk and stir until smooth and glossy.

4. Drizzle the chocolate sauce over the pear, top with a swirl of cream and a chocolate leaf if liked. Serve at once.

TWO

1. Using a sharp knife, halve the trifle sponges horizontally. Sandwich together with the chocolate and hazelnut spread. Place in a serving dish.

2. Put the ice cream into the pear hollows and place ice cream side down on the trifle sponges. Keep cool.

3. Place the chocolate in a bowl with the butter. Microwave on HIGH for 2 minutes to melt. Add the milk and stir until smooth and glossy.

4. Drizzle the chocolate sauce over the pears, top with a swirl of cream and a chocolate leaf if liked. Serve at once.

PEAR DÉLICE

Pears, strawberries and chocolate make an unbeatable combination in this quickly prepared dessert.

ONE		TWO
1	**ripe dessert pears**	2
5 ml/1 tsp	**lemon juice**	10 ml/2 tsp
2	**small scoops strawberry ice cream**	4
3	**fresh strawberries, hulled and sliced**	6
25 g/1 oz	**plain chocolate**	50 g/2 oz
15 g/½ oz	**butter**	25 g/1 oz
15 ml/1 tbsp	**milk**	30 ml/2 tbsp

ONE

1. Peel, halve and core the pear. Toss in the lemon juice and place in a serving dish.

2. Top with the strawberry ice cream and sliced strawberries. Keep cool.

3. Place the chocolate in a bowl with the milk and microwave on HIGH for 1–1¼ minutes to melt. Add the milk and stir until smooth and glossy.

4. Spoon over the pear dessert and serve at once.

TWO

1. Peel, halve and core the pears. Toss in the lemon juice and place in a serving dish.

2. Top with the strawberry ice cream and sliced strawberries. Keep cool.

3. Place the chocolate in a bowl with the milk and microwave on HIGH for 2 minutes to melt. Add the milk and stir until smooth and glossy.

4. Spoon over the pear dessert and serve at once.

ORANGE MOUSSE

Light, fluffy and refreshing orange mousse is the perfect dessert to serve after a hearty main course.

ONE		TWO
1	**eggs, separated**	2
5 ml/1 tsp	**finely grated orange rind**	10 ml/2 tsp
5 ml/1 tsp	**powdered gelatine**	10 ml/2 tsp
30 ml/2 tbsp	**water**	45 ml/3 tbsp
25 ml/5 tsp	**orange syrup**	50 ml/2 fl oz
50 ml/2 fl oz	**whipping cream**	100 ml/4 fl oz
	orange slices, to decorate	

ONE

1. Whisk the egg yolk and orange rind until pale and fluffy.
2. Place the water in a small bowl and sprinkle over the gelatine, leave for about 5 minutes until spongy. Microwave on HIGH for ¼–½ minute until clear and dissolved.
3. Fold the gelatine mixture and syrup into the egg mixture and leave until just beginning to set.
4. Whisk the egg white until it stands in stiff peaks. Whip the cream until it stands in soft peaks.
5. Fold the cream and egg white into the orange mixture, blending well. Spoon into a serving dish and chill until set. Decorate with orange slices.

TWO

1. Whisk the egg yolks and orange rind until pale and fluffy.
2. Place the water in a small bowl and sprinkle over the gelatine, leave for about 5 minutes until spongy. Microwave on HIGH for ¼–½ minute until clear and dissolved.
3. Fold the gelatine mixture and syrup into the egg mixture and leave until just beginning to set.
4. Whisk the egg whites until they stand in stiff peaks. Whip the cream until it stands in soft peaks.
5. Fold the cream and egg whites into the orange mixture, blending well. Spoon into a serving dish and chill until set. Decorate with orange slices.

CHOCOLATE SHELL MOUSSES

The 'shell' in this recipe is a ready-made chocolate shell that can be bought at many good delicatessens or selected supermarkets. However, it isn't essential; if unavailable spoon the mousse into a small serving dish instead.

ONE		TWO
25 g/1 oz	**plain chocolate**	50 g/2 oz
	small knob of butter	
1	**eggs, separated**	2
1	**ready-made chocolate shells**	2
	grated white chocolate, to decorate	

ONE

1. Place the chocolate in a bowl and microwave on HIGH for ½–1 minute until melted. Stir in the butter, blending well.
2. Add the egg yolk and beat well.
3. Whisk the egg white until it stands in stiff peaks and fold into the chocolate mixture using a metal spoon. Spoon into the chocolate shell and chill until set.
4. Serve chilled, sprinkled with a little grated white chocolate.

TWO

1. Place the chocolate in a bowl and microwave on HIGH for 1–1½ minutes until melted. Stir in the butter, blending well.
2. Add the egg yolks and beat well.
3. Whisk the egg whites until they stand in stiff peaks and fold into the chocolate mixture using a metal spoon. Spoon into the chocolate shells and chill until set.
4. Serve chilled, sprinkled with a little grated white chocolate.

COFFEE AND TIA MARIA MOUSSE

Light and airy – coffee and Tia Maria mousse is both simple and sophisticated. Decorate with whipped cream and candied coffee beans for a special occasion.

ONE		TWO
1	**eggs, separated**	2
25 g/1 oz	**caster sugar**	50 g/2 oz
45 ml/3 tbsp	**water**	90 ml/6 tbsp
5 ml/1 tsp	**instant coffee granules**	10 ml/2 tsp
5 ml/1 tsp	**powdered gelatine**	10 ml/2 tsp
45 ml/3 tbsp	**double cream**	90 ml/6 tbsp
5–10 ml/1–2 tsp	**Tia Maria liqueur**	10–20 ml/2–4 tsp
	whipped cream and candied coffee beans, to decorate (optional)	

ONE

1. Whisk the egg yolk with the sugar until thick and creamy.

2. Mix the water with the coffee in a small bowl. Sprinkle over the gelatine and leave to soak for about 5 minutes until spongy. Microwave on HIGH for ½–¾ minute until clear and dissolved.

3. Stir into the egg and sugar mixture, blending well.

4. Whip the cream until it stands in soft peaks and fold into the coffee mixture with the Tia Maria, blending well.

5. Whisk the egg white until it stands in soft peaks. Fold into the mousse with a metal spoon. Pour gently into a serving dish and chill until set.

6. Decorate with whipped cream and candied coffee beans, before serving, if liked.

TWO

1. Whisk the egg yolks with the sugar until thick and creamy.

2. Mix the water with the coffee in a small bowl. Sprinkle over the gelatine and leave to soak for about 5 minutes until spongy. Microwave on HIGH for ½–1 minute until clear and dissolved.

3. Stir into the egg and sugar mixture, blending well.

4. Whip the cream until it stands in soft peaks and fold into the coffee mixture with the Tia Maria, blending well.

5. Whisk the egg whites until they stand in soft peaks. Fold into the mousse with a metal spoon. Pour gently into a serving dish and chill until set.

6. Decorate with whipped cream and candied coffee beans, before serving, if liked.

GOOSEBERRY FOOL

A fruit fool is a quick and easy dessert that can be made with almost any fruit purée. Gooseberry has that special tartness that offsets and complements the richness of custard and cream. Serve with crisp dessert biscuits.

ONE		TWO
225 g/8 oz	**gooseberries, topped and tailed**	450 g/1 lb
7.5 ml/1½ tsp	**water**	15 ml/1 tbsp
7.5 ml/1½ tsp	**clear honey**	15 ml/1 tbsp
7.5 ml/1½ tsp	**caster sugar**	15 ml/1 tbsp
45 ml/3 tbsp	**double cream**	75 ml/5 tbsp
150 ml/¼ pint	**Speedy Custard Sauce (see page 100)**	300 ml/½ pint
	chopped nuts, to decorate	

ONE

1. Place the gooseberries, water, honey and sugar in a bowl. Cover and microwave on HIGH for 2–3 minutes until tender. Allow to cool then purée in a blender or push through a fine sieve.

2. Whip the cream until it stands in soft peaks and fold into the gooseberry purée with the custard. Spoon into a serving bowl and chill thoroughly.

3. Serve chilled, sprinkled with a few chopped nuts.

TWO

1. Place the gooseberries, water, honey and sugar in a bowl. Cover and microwave on HIGH for 4 minutes until tender. Allow to cool then purée in a blender or push through a fine sieve.

2. Whip the cream until it stands in soft peaks and fold into the gooseberry purée with the custard. Spoon into a serving bowl and chill thoroughly.

3. Serve chilled, sprinkled with a few chopped nuts.

BANANAS RHUMBA

A recipe from Barbados where rum is an everyday and essential ingredient. Serve with cream or ice cream.

ONE		TWO
1	**large, firm bananas**	2
7.5 ml/1½ tsp	**lemon juice**	15 ml/1 tbsp
15 ml/1 tbsp	**orange juice**	30 ml/2 tbsp
7.5 ml/1½ tsp	**golden syrup**	15 ml/1 tbsp
15 ml/1 tbsp	**dark rum**	30 ml/2 tbsp
15 g/½ oz	**unsalted butter**	25 g/1 oz
7 g/¼ oz	**flaked toasted almonds**	15 g/½ oz

ONE

1. Halve the banana lengthwise and place in a shallow dish. Brush with the lemon juice.

2. Mix the orange juice with the golden syrup and rum, pour over the banana and dot with the butter.

3. Cover loosely and microwave on HIGH for 1–1½ minutes. Sprinkle with the almonds and serve at once.

TWO

1. Halve the bananas lengthwise and place in a shallow dish. Brush with the lemon juice.

2. Mix the orange juice with the golden syrup and rum, pour over the bananas and dot with the butter.

3. Cover loosely and microwave on HIGH for 2–3 minutes. Sprinkle with the almonds and serve at once.

See photograph on page 118·119

ICE CREAM WITH CHOCOLATE SAUCE

There are so many unusual and exotic flavours of ice cream available today that plain vanilla can seem a trifle ordinary. Lift it into the luxury class with a little chocolate sauce and it soon surpasses the rest!

ONE		TWO
25 g/1 oz	**plain chocolate**	50 g/2 oz
15 g/½ oz	**unsalted butter**	25 g/1 oz
15 ml/1 tbsp	**milk**	30 ml/2 tbsp
2	**scoops vanilla ice cream**	4
	chopped nuts, to decorate	

ONE

1. Place the chocolate in a bowl with the butter and microwave on HIGH for 1–1¼ minutes to melt.

2. Add the milk and stir until smooth and glossy.

3. Place the ice cream in a serving dish and spoon over the warm chocolate sauce.

4. Decorate with a few chopped nuts and serve at once.

TWO

1. Place the chocolate in a bowl with the butter and microwave on HIGH for 2 minutes to melt.

2. Add the milk and stir until smooth and glossy.

3. Place the ice cream in two serving dishes and spoon over the warm chocolate sauce.

4. Decorate with a few chopped nuts and serve at once.

VARIATIONS

ICE CREAM WITH BUTTERSCOTCH SAUCE

To make a butterscotch sauce to serve 2, place 20 g/¾ oz butter and 100 g/4 oz soft light brown sugar in a jug. Microwave on HIGH for 1–1¼ minutes to melt. Stir in 75 ml/5 tbsp evaporated milk and microwave on HIGH for ½–1 minute. Stir in 10 ml/2 tsp brandy, if liked. Pour over ice cream and decorate with chopped nuts.

RASPBERRY SUNDAE

Sundaes are quick, colourful and popular at all times. They are also very simple to make, all you need is ice cream, a tangy fruit sauce and lashings of cream.

ONE		TWO
50 g/2 oz	**raspberries, hulled**	100 g/4 oz
15 ml/1 tbsp	**grenadine fruit syrup**	30 ml/2 tbsp
7 g/¼ oz	**caster sugar**	15 g/½ oz
2	**scoops vanilla ice cream**	4
7 g/¼ oz	**toasted flaked almonds**	15 g/½ oz
	whipped cream	

ONE

1. Reserve a few raspberries for decoration and place the rest in a bowl. Add the grenadine fruit syrup and sugar, blending well. Cover and microwave on HIGH for 1–1½ minutes until very soft. Push through a nylon sieve or purée in a blender and leave until cold.

2. To serve, place the ice cream in a serving dish. Pour over the raspberry sauce and sprinkle with the almonds.

3. Decorate with a whirl of whipped cream.

TWO

1. Reserve a few raspberries for decoration and place the rest in a bowl. Add the grenadine fruit syrup and sugar, blending well. Cover and microwave on HIGH for 1½–2 minutes until very soft. Push through a nylon sieve or purée in a blender and leave until cold.

2. To serve, place the ice cream in a serving dish. Pour over the raspberry sauce and sprinkle with the almonds.

3. Decorate with a whirl of whipped cream.

See photograph on page 117

VARIATIONS

RASPBERRY AND PEACH RIPPLE SUNDAE

Prepare and cook as above but cook the raspberries in lemon syrup. Serve with scoops of raspberry ripple ice cream, peach halves and whipped cream.

LOGANBERRY AND BANANA SUNDAE

Use loganberries instead of raspberries; cook in orange syrup. Serve with vanilla ice cream, bananas and whipped cream.

REDCURRANT AND GRENADINE SUNDAE

Use redcurrants instead of raspberries; cook in grenadine syrup. Serve with strawberry ice cream, sponge fingers, sprigs of fresh redcurrants (dipped in egg white and caster sugar) and whipped cream.

CHOCOLATE FUDGE SUNDAE

The scrumptious chocolate fudge sauce for this sundae can be made up to 48 hours in advance then quickly reheated for serving.

ONE		TWO
20 g/¾ oz	**plain chocolate**	40 g/1½ oz
small knob	**butter**	20 g/¾ oz
25 ml/1 fl oz	**milk**	50 ml/2 fl oz
75 g/3 oz	**soft brown sugar**	175 g/6 oz
10 ml/2 tsp	**golden syrup**	20 ml/4 tsp
1	**large ripe bananas, peeled and sliced**	2
1	**peaches, peeled and sliced**	2
1	**scoops vanilla ice cream**	2
7 g/¼ oz	**chopped hazelnuts**	15 g/½ oz
	maraschino cherries, to decorate	

ONE

1. Place the chocolate in a bowl with the butter. Microwave on HIGH for ¾–1minute to melt, stirring twice.

2. Add the milk, sugar and golden syrup, blending well. Microwave on HIGH for 2–3 minutes, stirring every 1 minute until hot and bubbly.

3. To serve, place the banana and peach in a sundae glass. Top with the ice cream. Pour over the warm fudge sauce, sprinkle with the nuts, decorate with a cherry and serve at once.

TWO

1. Place the chocolate in a bowl with the butter. Microwave on HIGH for 1–1½ minutes to melt, stirring twice.

2. Add the milk, sugar and golden syrup, blending well. Microwave on HIGH for 3–4 minutes, stirring every 1 minute until hot and bubbly.

3. To serve, place the banana and peach in a sundae glass. Top with the ice cream. Pour over the warm fudge sauce, sprinkle with the nuts, decorate with a cherry and serve at once.

DANISH RØDGRØD

A Danish dessert of puréed berry fruits lightly thickened with cornflour. Chill then swirl with cream just before serving for a dramatic effect.

ONE		TWO
100 g/4 oz	**redcurrants or redcurrants and blackcurrants mixed, topped and tailed**	225 g/8 oz
50 g/2 oz	**raspberries, hulled**	100 g/4 oz
25 g/1 oz	**caster sugar**	50 g/2 oz
7 g/¼ oz	**cornflour**	15 g/½ oz
30 ml/2 tbsp	**double cream**	60 ml/4 tbsp

ONE

1. Place the redcurrants and raspberries in a bowl with the sugar. Cover and microwave on HIGH for 1½–2 minutes until tender. Purée in a blender or push through a fine nylon sieve.

2. Return to the bowl and add the cornflour blended to a smooth paste with a little cold water. Microwave on HIGH for 1–2 minutes until smooth and thickened, stirring three times. Allow to cool, stirring occasionally, to prevent a skin from forming.

3. Spoon into a serving dish and chill lightly. Swirl the cream on top to serve.

TWO

1. Place the redcurrants and raspberries in a bowl with the sugar. Cover and microwave on HIGH for 2–3 minutes until tender. Purée in a blender or push through a fine nylon sieve.

2. Return to the bowl and add the cornflour blended to a smooth paste with a little cold water. Microwave on HIGH for 1½–2 minutes until smooth and thickened, stirring three times. Allow to cool, stirring occasionally, to prevent a skin from forming.

3. Spoon into a serving dish and chill lightly. Swirl the cream on top to serve.

BAKED PEARS

Pears for cooking should be firm but ripe. Choose those that have started to soften at the stem end.

ONE		TWO
1	**firm ripe pears**	2
15 ml/1 tbsp	**brown sugar**	30 ml/2 tbsp
15 g/½ oz	**unsalted butter**	25 g/1 oz
	pinch of ground cinnamon or ginger	

ONE

1. Halve and core the pear. Arrange cut-side up in a small dish with the thin ends to the centre of the dish.

2. Sprinkle the cut surface with the sugar, dot with the butter and dust with the chosen spice.

3. Cover and microwave on HIGH for 2½–3½ minutes.

4. Allow to stand, covered, for 2 minutes before serving with whipped cream if liked.

TWO

1. Halve and core the pears. Arrange cut-side up in a small dish with the thin ends to the centre of the dish.

2. Sprinkle the cut surface with the sugar, dot with the butter and dust with the chosen spice.

3. Cover and microwave on HIGH for 4–6½ minutes.

4. Allow to stand, covered, for 2 minutes before serving with whipped cream if liked.

LAYERED RHUBARB CREAM

Layers of pink-tinged rhubarb cream and buttery nutty crumbs make up this inexpensive dessert.

ONE		TWO
100 g/4 oz	**rhubarb, trimmed and chopped**	225 g/8 oz
25 g/1 oz	**caster sugar**	50 g/2 oz
50 ml/2 fl oz	**double cream**	100 ml/4 fl oz
10 ml/2 tsp	**icing sugar**	20 ml/4 tsp
15 g/½ oz	**butter**	25 g/1 oz
15 g/½ oz	**soft brown sugar**	25 g/1 oz
40 g/1½ oz	**fresh white breadcrumbs**	75 g/3 oz
15 ml/1 tbsp	**chopped mixed nuts**	30 ml/2 tbsp
	mint sprigs, to decorate (optional)	

ONE

1. Place the rhubarb in a bowl with the sugar. Cover and microwave on HIGH for 3–3½ minutes until soft, stirring once. Purée in a blender or pass through a fine sieve.

2. Whip the cream with the icing sugar until it stands in soft peaks and fold into the rhubarb purée.

3. Place the butter, brown sugar and breadcrumbs in a bowl. Microwave on HIGH for 1–2 minutes until crisp and golden. Leave to cool then stir in the nuts.

4. To serve, layer the rhubarb cream and nutty crumbs in a dessert glass. Chill thoroughly.

TWO

1. Place the rhubarb in a bowl with the sugar. Cover and microwave on HIGH for 6–7 minutes until soft, stirring once. Purée in a blender or through a sieve.

2. Whip the cream with the icing sugar until it stands in soft peaks and fold into the rhubarb purée.

3. Place the butter, brown sugar and breadcrumbs in a bowl. Microwave on HIGH for 1½–2 minutes until crisp and golden. Leave to cool then stir in the nuts.

4. To serve, layer the rhubarb cream and nutty crumbs in two dessert glasses. Chill thoroughly.

WHIM WHAM

Whim Wham is a rather odd sounding traditional British dessert made with cream.

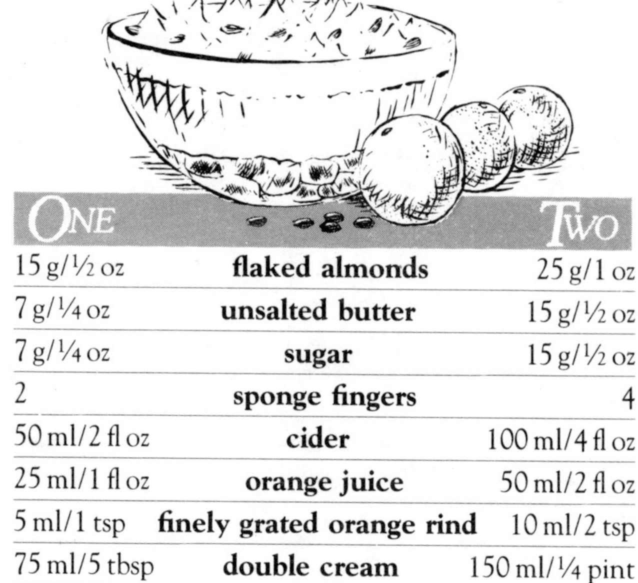

ONE		TWO
15 g/½ oz	**flaked almonds**	25 g/1 oz
7 g/¼ oz	**unsalted butter**	15 g/½ oz
7 g/¼ oz	**sugar**	15 g/½ oz
2	**sponge fingers**	4
50 ml/2 fl oz	**cider**	100 ml/4 fl oz
25 ml/1 fl oz	**orange juice**	50 ml/2 fl oz
5 ml/1 tsp	**finely grated orange rind**	10 ml/2 tsp
75 ml/5 tbsp	**double cream**	150 ml/¼ pint

ONE

1. Place the almonds and butter in a bowl and microwave on HIGH for 2½ minutes until golden. Stir in the sugar and microwave on HIGH for 2½–3 minutes until caramelised. Quickly pour onto a sheet of greaseproof paper and allow to cool.

2. Break the sponge fingers into large pieces and place in the bottom of a serving dish.

3. Mix the cider with the orange juice and pour over the sponge fingers. Sprinkle with half of the grated orange rind.

4. Whip the cream until it stands in soft peaks and swirl over the sponge fingers. Sprinkle with the remaining grated orange rind.

5. Break the caramelised almonds into pieces and sprinkle over the cream. Serve lightly chilled.

TWO

1. Place the almonds and butter in a bowl and microwave on HIGH for 3–4 minutes until golden. Stir in the sugar and microwave on HIGH for 3–4 minutes until caramelised. Quickly pour onto a sheet of greaseproof paper and allow to cool.

2. Break the sponge fingers into large pieces and place in the bottom of 2 serving dishes.

3. Mix the cider with the orange juice and pour over the sponge fingers. Sprinkle with half of the grated orange rind.

4. Whip the cream until it stands in soft peaks and spoon or swirl over the sponge fingers. Sprinkle with the remaining grated orange rind.

5. Break the caramelised almonds into pieces and sprinkle over the cream. Serve lightly chilled.

CRÈME CARAMELS

Creamy smooth and tantalisingly light Crème Caramels are popular desserts to serve after a hearty main course.

ONE		TWO
15 g/½ oz	**sugar**	25 g/1 oz
7.5 ml/1½ tsp	**water**	15 ml/1 tbsp
1	**eggs**	2
7 g/¼ oz	**caster sugar**	15 g/½ oz
150 ml/¼ pint	**milk**	300 ml/½ pint

ONE

1. Place the sugar and water in a small heat resistant bowl or jug and microwave on HIGH for 1–1½ minutes until golden brown. Pour into a large tea cup or a cocotte dish.

2. Whisk the egg with the caster sugar.

3. Place the milk in a jug and microwave on HIGH for 1 minute. Whisk into the egg mixture, blending well.

4. Strain over the caramel and microwave on LOW for 4–5 minutes until just set.

5. Allow to cool then chill until set.

6. To serve, unmould onto a serving dish.

TWO

1. Place the sugar and water in a small heat resistant bowl or jug and microwave on HIGH for 2–2½ minutes until golden brown. Pour into 2 large tea cups or cocottes.

2. Whisk the eggs with the caster sugar.

3. Place the milk in a jug and microwave on HIGH for 2 minutes. Whisk into the egg mixture, blending well.

4. Strain over the caramel and microwave on LOW for 9–10 minutes until just set.

5. Allow to cool then chill until set.

6. To serve, unmould onto a serving dish.

COOK'S TIP

Crème Caramels are made easily in the microwave. Cook until just set, if overcooked the custard will be curdled and unappetising.

APRICOTS AND CURAÇAO

Looking for a dessert in a hurry? Then look no further than your fruit bowl – slice apricots, peaches or nectarines into a bowl, add a dash of a compatible and favourite liqueur and you have the makings of a fine feast.

ONE		TWO
3	**fresh apricots, peeled, stoned and sliced**	6
15 ml/1 tbsp	**curaçao liqueur**	30 ml/2 tbsp

ONE

1. Place the apricot slices in a serving dish. Cover and microwave on HIGH for 1 minute.

2. Add the curaçao and mix well to blend.

3. Serve at once while still warm, with a scoop of ice cream, if liked.

TWO

1. Place the apricot slices in a serving dish. Cover and microwave on HIGH for 2 minutes.

2. Add the curaçao and mix well to blend.

3. Serve at once while still warm, with a scoop of ice cream, if liked.

PINEAPPLE, BANANA AND DATE FLAMBÉ

A microwave dessert that is flamed traditionally just before serving.

ONE		TWO
1	**firm bananas, peeled and thickly sliced**	2
½	**small pineapple, peeled, cored and cut into 2.5 cm/1 inch pieces**	1
25 g/1 oz	**fresh dates, stoned and cut into strips**	50 g/2 oz
7 g/¼ oz	**butter**	15 g/½ oz
15 g/½ oz	**demerara sugar**	25 g/1 oz
10 ml/2 tsp	**pineapple juice**	20 ml/4 tsp
	pinch of ground mixed spice	
15 ml/1 tbsp	**chopped mixed nuts**	30 ml/2 tbsp
30 ml/2 tbsp	**dark rum**	45 ml/3 tbsp

ONE

1. Place the bananas, pineapple and dates in a shallow dish.

2. Place the butter in a bowl and microwave on HIGH for ¼ minute to melt. Stir in the sugar, pineapple juice and spice, blending well. Pour over the prepared fruits.

3. Cover and microwave on HIGH for 2–3 minutes until hot and bubbly. Sprinkle with the nuts.

4. Put the rim in a small saucepan and heat gently until warm. Carefully ignite, then pour over the fruit.

TWO

1. Place the bananas, pineapple and dates in a shallow dish.

2. Place the butter in a bowl and microwave on HIGH for ½ minute to melt. Stir in the sugar, pineapple juice and spice, blending well. Pour over the prepared fruits.

3. Cover and microwave on HIGH for 4–5 minutes until hot and bubbly. Sprinkle with the nuts.

4. Put the rum in a small saucepan and heat gently until warm. Carefully ignite, then pour over the fruit.

DATE BAKED APPLES

Baked apples stuffed with dates and sugar make delicious eating at any time of the year.

ONE		TWO
1	**medium cooking apples**	2
1	**large dried dates, stoned and chopped**	2
15 ml/1 tbsp	**demerara sugar**	30 ml/2 tbsp
7 g/¼ oz	**unsalted butter**	15 g/½ oz
25 ml/1 fl oz	**cider**	50 ml/2 fl oz

ONE

1. Wash the apple and remove the core. Using a sharp knife, cut a slit around the middle of the apple to prevent the skin from bursting during cooking. Stand upright in a small dish.

2. Mix the dates with the sugar and use to stuff the apple. Pour the cider around the apple. Cover and microwave on HIGH for 2–3 minutes until just tender.

3. Serve at once with custard or cream.

TWO

1. Wash and remove the core from the apples. Using a sharp knife, cut a slit around the middle of each apple to prevent the skin from bursting during cooking. Stand upright in a small shallow dish.

2. Mix the dates with the sugar and use to stuff the apples. Pour the cider around the apple. Cover and microwave on HIGH for 5–6 minutes until just tender.

3. Serve at once with custard or cream.

See photograph on page 118·119

Red fruits salad (page 106) and Raspberry sundae (page 112).

OVERLEAF

From left: Lemon zabaglione (page 126), Simple lemon cheesecake (page 122), Date baked apples (recipe above), Peach macaroons (page 122) and Bananas rhumba (page 111).

DAMSON COMPOTE

A soothing warm fruit compote made with damsons, sherry, sliced oranges and sultanas. Delicious served with a swirl of soured cream or natural yogurt.

ONE		TWO
15 g/½ oz	**sultanas**	25 g/1 oz
45 ml/3 tbsp	**medium dry sherry or Madeira**	75 ml/5 tbsp
10 ml/2 tsp	**dark brown sugar**	20 ml/4 tsp
1	**small oranges, peeled, pith removed and segmented**	2
1	**cinnamon stick**	1
75 g/3 oz	**damsons, halved and stoned**	175 g/6 oz

ONE

1. Place the sultanas, sherry or Madeira, any juices from preparing the oranges and the cinnamon stick in a bowl. Cover and microwave on HIGH for ½ minute. Leave to cool, covered.

2. Remove and discard the cinnamon stick. Add the orange slices and damsons, blending well. Cover and microwave on HIGH for 1½–2 minutes, stirring once. Leave to stand, covered, for 3 minutes.

3. Serve at once with a swirl of soured cream, if liked.

TWO

1. Place the sultanas, sherry, or Madeira, any juices from preparing the oranges and the cinnamon stick in a bowl. Cover and microwave on HIGH for 1 minute. Leave to cool, covered.

2. Remove and discard the cinnamon stick. Add the orange slices and damsons, blending well. Cover and microwave on HIGH for 2–3 minutes, stirring once. Leave to stand, covered, for 3 minutes.

3. Serve at once with a swirl of soured cream, if liked.

From above: Rice and raisin pudding (page 124), Marmalade suet pudding (page 125) and Mini upside down pudding (page 125).

ORCHARD DRIED FRUIT SALAD

Almost any mixture of dried fruits can be used in this recipe – pears, apples, prunes, figs, dates, raisins or bananas.

ONE		TWO
100 g/4 oz	**mixed dried fruits**	225 g/8 oz
50 ml/2 fl oz	**cold tea**	100 ml/4 fl oz
50 ml/2 fl oz	**water**	100 ml/4 fl oz
15 ml/1 tbsp	**clear honey**	30 ml/2 tbsp
5 ml/1 tsp	**lemon juice**	10 ml/2 tsp
1	**small cinnamon stick**	1
2	**whole cloves**	2
7.5 ml/1½ tsp	**brandy (optional)**	15 ml/1 tbsp
15 g/½ oz	**blanched almonds**	25 g/1 oz

ONE

1. Mix the fruits with the tea, water, honey, lemon juice, cinnamon stick and cloves in a bowl. Cover and leave to soak for 2 hours.

2. Microwave on HIGH for 4–5 minutes until the fruit is tender, stirring twice.

3. Remove and discard the cinnamon stick and cloves. Add the brandy, if liked and the almonds, blending well. Re-cover and leave to stand for 5 minutes.

4. Serve warm or cold with cream, yogurt or ice cream.

TWO

1. Mix the fruits with the tea, water, honey, lemon juice, cinnamon stick and cloves in a bowl. Cover and leave to soak for 2 hours.

2. Microwave on HIGH for 8–10 minutes until the fruit is tender, stirring twice.

3. Remove and discard the cinnamon stick and cloves. Add the brandy, if liked, and the almonds, blending well. Re-cover and leave to stand for 5 minutes.

4. Serve warm or cold with cream, yogurt or ice cream.

SIMPLE LEMON CHEESECAKE

A creamy smooth cheesecake made quickly and effectively with custard, cream cheese and jelly.

ONE		TWO
15 g/½ oz	**butter**	25 g/1 oz
2	**digestive biscuits, crushed**	4
3	**lemon jelly cubes**	6
5 ml/1 tsp	**finely grated lemon rind**	10 ml/2 tsp
10 ml/2 tsp	**lemon juice**	20 ml/4 tsp
30 ml/2 tbsp	**water**	60 ml/4 tbsp
50 g/2 oz	**cream cheese**	100 g/4 oz
150 ml/¼ pint	**Speedy Custard Sauce (see page 100)**	300 ml/½ pint
	whipped cream and fresh fruit, to decorate (optional)	

ONE

1. Place the butter in a bowl and microwave on HIGH for ¼–½ minute to melt. Stir in the biscuit crumbs, coating well.

2. Use to line the base of a 15 cm/5 inch diameter small deep loose-bottomed tartlet tin. Chill until set.

3. Place the jelly cubes, lemon rind, lemon juice and water in a bowl. Microwave on HIGH for 1 minute to dissolve, stirring once.

4. Beat the cheese until soft then stir in the jelly mixture and the custard, blending well. Leave to cool until syrupy then pour over the biscuit base. Chill.

5. To serve, remove from the tins and decorate with cream and fruit, if liked.

TWO

1. Place the butter in a bowl and microwave on HIGH for ½ minute to melt. Stir in the biscuit crumbs, coating well.

2. Use to line the base of 2 15 cm/5 inch diameter small deep loose-bottomed tartlet tins. Chill until set.

3. Place the jelly cubes, lemon rind, lemon juice and water in a bowl. Microwave on HIGH for 1½ minutes to dissolve, stirring once.

4. Beat the cheese until soft then stir in the jelly mixture and custard, blending well. Leave to cool until syrupy then pour over the biscuit base. Chill until set.

5. To serve, remove from the tins and decorate with cream and fruit, if liked.

See photograph on page 118-119

PEACH MACAROONS

I first tested this recipe with macaroon biscuits and was delighted with the result. Later, in a fit of extravagance, I tried using Amaretti di Saronno biscuits and adored it.

ONE		TWO
1	**firm peach (white if available), peeled, halved and stoned**	2
2	**macaroon or Amaretti di Saronno biscuits**	4
7 g/¼ oz	**flaked almonds**	15 g/½ oz
7.5 ml/1½ tsp	**clear honey**	15 ml/1 tbsp
45 ml/3 tbsp	**dry white wine**	75 ml/5 tbsp

ONE

1. Place the peach halves in a shallow dish.

2. Coarsely crush the biscuits and mix with the almonds. Spoon into the peach cavities and trickle over the honey.

3. Spoon a little of the wine over the biscuit mixture to moisten slightly then pour the remainder around the peaches.

4. Partially cover and microwave on HIGH for 1–1½ minutes. Serve hot or cold with cream, if liked.

TWO

1. Place the peach halves in a shallow dish.

2. Coarsely crush the biscuits and mix with the almonds. Spoon into the peach cavities and trickle over the honey.

3. Spoon a little of the wine over the biscuit mixture

to moisten slightly then pour the remainder around the peaches.

4. Partially cover and microwave on HIGH for 2–3 minutes. Serve hot or cold with cream, if liked.

See photograph on page 118-119

APPLE AND ORANGE CRUMBLE

A traditional oven-baked favourite made in a trice using the microwave. Brown under a preheated grill for a golden crust, if liked.

ONE		TWO
100 g/4 oz	**peeled, cored and sliced dessert apples**	225 g/8 oz
5 ml/1 tsp	**finely grated orange rind**	10 ml/2 tsp
25 g/1 oz	**butter**	50 g/2 oz
40 g/1½ oz	**plain flour**	75 g/3 oz
15 g/½ oz	**soft brown sugar**	25 g/1 oz

ONE

1. Place the apples in a small heatproof dish and sprinkle with the orange rind.
2. Rub the butter into the flour until the mixture resembles fine breadcrumbs then stir in the sugar, blending well.
3. Spoon on top of the fruit and microwave on HIGH for 3½–4 minutes until cooked. Brown under a preheated grill, if liked.

TWO

1. Place the apples in a small heatproof dish and sprinkle with the orange rind.
2. Rub the butter into the flour until the mixture resembles fine breadcrumbs then stir in the sugar, blending well.
3. Spoon on top of the fruit and microwave on HIGH for 7–8 minutes until cooked. Brown under a preheated grill, if liked.

ORANGE SEMOLINA PUDDING

A creamy milk pudding flavoured with orange zest. Eat this nursery-style pudding warm during autumn and winter months.

ONE		TWO
300 ml/½ pint	**milk**	600 ml/1 pint
30 ml/2 tbsp	**semolina**	60 ml/4 tbsp
5 ml/1 tsp	**finely grated orange rind**	10 ml/2 tsp
15 ml/1 tbsp	**caster sugar**	30 ml/2 tbsp

ONE

1. Place the milk, semolina, orange rind and sugar in a bowl, blending well.
2. Microwave on HIGH for 3 minutes or until the milk boils.
3. Stir well, cover and microwave on HIGH for 1 minute.
4. Reduce the power setting and microwave on LOW for 5–7 minutes until cooked, stirring three times.
5. Leave to stand, covered, for 5 minutes before serving.

TWO

1. Place the milk, semolina, orange rind and sugar in a bowl, blending well.
2. Microwave on HIGH for 5–6 minutes or until the milk boils.
3. Stir well, cover and microwave on HIGH for 2 minutes.
4. Reduce the power setting and microwave on LOW for 10–14 minutes until cooked, stirring three times.
5. Leave to stand, covered, for 5 minutes before serving.

COOK'S TIP

To make Lemon Semolina Pudding, use lemon rind instead of orange rind. Alternatively omit the orange rind and serve with a spoonful of your favourite jam.

RICE AND RAISIN PUDDING

Few puddings are as popular as this creamy and comforting nursery favourite.

ONE		TWO
25 g/1 oz	**short grain rice**	50 g/2 oz
250 ml/8 fl oz	**milk**	475 ml/16 fl oz
50 ml/2 fl oz	**evaporated milk**	100 ml/4 fl oz
15 g/½ oz	**brown sugar**	25 g/1 oz
25 g/1 oz	**raisins**	50 g/2 oz
	pinch of ground nutmeg	

ONE

1. Place the rice, milk, evaporated milk and sugar in a bowl. Cover and microwave on HIGH for 3 minutes, stirring once.

2. Reduce the power setting to MEDIUM and microwave for a further 18 minutes, stirring once halfway through the cooking time.

3. Stir in the raisins and nutmeg, blending well. Cover and leave to stand for 5 minutes before serving.

TWO

1. Place the rice, milk, evaporated milk and sugar in a bowl. Cover and microwave on HIGH for 5 minutes, stirring once.

2. Reduce the power setting to MEDIUM and microwave for a further 27 minutes, stirring once halfway through the cooking time.

3. Stir in the raisins and nutmeg, blending well. Cover and leave to stand for 5 minutes before serving.

STORECUPBOARD STANDBY

A storecupboard favourite made simply in the microwave, try adding chopped nuts or dried fruit such as apricots or dates as a healthy variation.

See photograph on page 120

RED TOP CASTLE PUDDINGS

Red top castle puddings are individual sponge puddings that are cooked in small cups or glass dariole pudding moulds and topped with raspberry or strawberry jam.

ONE		TWO
15 ml/1 tbsp	**raspberry or strawberry jam**	30 ml/2 tbsp
25 g/1 oz	**butter**	50 g/2 oz
25 g/1 oz	**caster sugar**	50 g/2 oz
	few drops vanilla essence	
½	**egg, beaten**	1
25 g/1 oz	**self-raising flour**	50 g/2 oz
5 ml/1 tsp	**milk**	10–15 ml/2–3 tsp

ONE

1. Place the jam in the base of a greased cup or glass dariole mould.

2. Cream the butter and sugar until light and fluffy. Add the vanilla essence and egg, beating well to blend. Fold in the flour and milk.

3. Spoon into the cup or mould over the jam. Microwave on HIGH for 1½–2 minutes. Leave to stand for 5 minutes before turning out onto a plate to serve. Serve hot with custard, if liked.

TWO

1. Place the jam in the base of two greased cups or glass dariole moulds.

2. Cream the butter and sugar until light and fluffy. Add the vanilla essence and egg, beating well to blend. Fold in the flour and milk.

3. Spoon into the cups or moulds over the jam. Microwave on HIGH for 3–4 minutes. Leave to stand for 5 minutes before turning out onto plates to serve. Serve hot with custard, if liked.

MINI UPSIDE DOWN PUDDING

Light as air sponge puddings that when turned out reveal a pineapple and cherry topping. Serve hot or cold with custard or cream.

ONE		TWO
5 ml/1 tsp	**demerara sugar**	10 ml/2 tsp
1	**canned pineapple rings**	2
1	**glacé cherries**	2
25 g/1 oz	**butter**	50 g/2 oz
25 g/1 oz	**caster sugar**	50 g/2 oz
	few drops vanilla essence	
½	**egg, beaten**	1
25 g/1 oz	**self-raising flour**	50 g/2 oz
5 ml/1 tsp	**milk**	10 ml/2 tsp

ONE

1. Sprinkle the base of a greased tea cup or very small bowl with the sugar. Place the pineapple ring in the base with the cherry in the centre.

2. Cream the butter and sugar until light and fluffy. Add the vanilla essence and egg, beating well to blend. Fold in the flour and milk.

3. Spoon into the cup or bowl over the pineapple. Microwave on HIGH for 1½–2¼ minutes. Leave to stand for 5 minutes before turning out onto a plate to serve. Serve hot or cold with custard or cream, if liked.

TWO

1. Sprinkle the base of two greased tea cups or small round bowls with the sugar. Place the pineapple rings in the base with the cherries in the centres.

2. Cream the butter and sugar until light and fluffy. Add the vanilla essence and egg, beating well to blend. Fold in the flour and milk.

3. Spoon into the cups or bowls over the pineapple. Microwave on HIGH for 3–4½ minutes. Leave to stand for 5 minutes before turning out onto plates to serve. Serve hot or cold with custard or cream, if liked.

See photograph on page 120

MARMALADE SUET PUDDING

A steamed suet pudding with a rich marmalade crown. Serve with pouring custard.

ONE		TWO
15 ml/1 tbsp	**orange marmalade**	30 ml/2 tbsp
25 g/1 oz	**self-raising flour**	50 g/2 oz
15 g/1 oz	**shredded suet**	25 g/1 oz
15 g/½ oz	**caster sugar**	25 g/1 oz
	few drops vanilla essence	
15 ml/1 tbsp	**beaten egg**	30 ml/2 tbsp
25 ml/1 fl oz	**milk**	50 ml/2 fl oz

ONE

1. Place the marmalade in the base of a greased teacup or very small bowl.

2. Beat the flour with the suet, sugar, vanilla essence, egg and milk, to make a smooth soft batter.

3. Spoon into the cup or bowl over the marmalade. Cover and microwave on HIGH for 1¼–1¾ minutes or until the pudding rises to the top of the cup or jug. Leave to stand for 5 minutes before turning out onto a plate to serve.

TWO

1. Place the marmalade in the base of 2 greased teacups or very small bowls.

2. Beat the flour with the suet, sugar, vanilla essence, egg and milk, to make a smooth soft batter.

3. Spoon into the cups or bowls over the marmalade. Cover and microwave on HIGH for 2½–3½ minutes or until the pudding rises to the top of the cup or jug. Leave to stand for 5 minutes before turning out onto a plate to serve.

COOK'S TIP

Try using lemon or lime marmalade instead of orange.

See photograph on page 120

BREAD AND BUTTER PUDDING

A scrumptious pudding to make with leftover bread. Place under a preheated grill to crisp and brown before serving.

ONE		TWO
2	**slices white bread, crusts removed**	4
25 g/1 oz	**butter**	50 g/2 oz
20 g/¾ oz	**sultanas**	40 g/1½ oz
1	**eggs, beaten**	2
15 g/½ oz	**caster sugar**	25 g/1 oz
150 ml/¼ pint	**milk**	300 ml/½ pint
	few drops of vanilla essence	
	ground nutmeg	

ONE

1. Lightly grease a 450 ml/¾ pint pie dish.

2. Spread the bread slices with the butter and cut into triangles. Layer in the pie dish with the sultanas.

3. Beat the eggs with the sugar, blending well. Place the milk in a jug and microwave on HIGH for ¼–½ minute until hot. Pour into the egg mixture with a little vanilla essence to taste. Pour over the bread slices and microwave on HIGH, uncovered, for 1½ minutes.

4. Press the bread down into the egg mixture and leave to stand for 3 minutes. Microwave on HIGH, uncovered, for a further 2 minutes. Leave to stand for 10 minutes.

5. Microwave on HIGH, uncovered, for a further 1–2 minutes until the custard has set.

6. Sprinkle with nutmeg. Serve hot or warm.

TWO

1. Lightly grease a 900 ml/1½ pint pie dish.

2. Spread the bread slices with the butter and cut into triangles. Layer in the pie dish with the sultanas.

3. Beat the eggs with the sugar, blending well. Place the milk in a jug and microwave on HIGH for ½–¾ minute until hot. Pour into the egg mixture with a little vanilla essence to taste. Pour over the bread slices and microwave on HIGH, uncovered, for 1½ minutes.

4. Press the bread down into the egg mixture and leave to stand for 3 minutes. Microwave on HIGH, uncovered, for a further 3½ minutes. Leave to stand for 10 minutes.

5. Microwave on HIGH, uncovered, for a further 2–3 minutes until the custard has set.

6. Sprinkle with nutmeg. Serve hot or warm.

LEMON ZABAGLIONE

Light, airy and sophisticated – serve with langue de chat biscuits or sponge fingers.

ONE		TWO
1	**egg yolks**	2
15 ml/1 tbsp	**caster sugar**	30 ml/2 tbsp
30 ml/2 tbsp	**Marsala or sweet sherry**	60 ml/2 tbsp
2.5 ml/½ tsp	**finely grated lemon rind**	5 ml/1 tsp

ONE

1. Using an electric beater whisk the egg yolk and sugar until thick and creamy.

2. Place the Marsala or sherry and lemon rind in a small bowl and microwave on HIGH for ¼–½ minute until just boiling.

3. Pour onto the egg mixture and whisk until thickened. Microwave on LOW for ½ minute then whisk for about 3–4 minutes until thick and frothy.

TWO

1. Using an electric beater whisk the egg yolks and sugar until thick and creamy.

2. Place the Marsala or sherry and lemon rind in a small bowl and microwave on HIGH for ¼–½ minute until just boiling.

3. Pour onto the egg mixture and whisk until thickened. Microwave on LOW for ½–1 minute then whisk for about 3–4 minutes until thick and frothy.

See photograph on page 118·119

GINGER SPONGE WITH ORANGE CUSTARD

Steamed sponges still seem magical as they rise before your very eyes in the microwave.

ONE		TWO
25 g/1 oz	**butter**	50 g/2 oz
25 g/1 oz	**caster sugar**	50 g/2 oz
½	**egg, beaten**	1
25 g/1 oz	**self-raising flour**	50 g/2 oz
2.5 ml/½ tsp	**ground ginger**	5 ml/1 tsp
15 ml/1 tbsp	**orange juice or syrup**	30 ml/2 tbsp
150 ml/¼ pint	**hot Speedy Custard Sauce (see page 100)**	300 ml/½ pint
2.5 ml/½ tsp	**finely grated orange rind**	5 ml/1 tsp

ONE

1. Cream the butter with the sugar until light and fluffy. Beat in the egg, blending well. Fold in the flour and ginger with a metal spoon and stir in half of the orange juice or syrup.

2. Lightly grease a teacup or very small bowl and add the sponge mixture. Cover loosely with cling film and microwave on HIGH for 1½–2 minutes until well risen and cooked. Allow to stand for 2 minutes.

3. Mix the hot custard sauce with the remaining orange juice or syrup and orange rind, blending well. Turn the pudding out and spoon over the custard.

TWO

1. Cream the butter with the sugar until light and fluffy. Beat in the egg, blending well. Fold in the flour and ginger with a metal spoon and stir in the orange juice or syrup, blending well.

2. Lightly grease 2 teacups or very small bowls and add the sponge mixture. Cover loosely with cling film and microwave on HIGH for 3–4 minutes until well risen and cooked. Allow to stand for 2 minutes.

3. Mix the hot custard sauce with the remaining orange juice or syrup and orange rind, blending well. Turn the puddings out and spoon over the custard.

BLACKCURRANT AND KIWI KISSEL

A refreshing light dessert of puréed blackcurrants cooked in honey and topped with paper thin slices of kiwi fruit.

ONE		TWO
100 g/4 oz	**blackcurrants, topped and tailed**	225 g/8 oz
15 ml/1 tbsp	**clear honey**	30 ml/2 tbsp
5 ml/1 tsp	**lemon juice**	10 ml/2 tsp
60 ml/4 tbsp	**water**	120 ml/8 tbsp
7 g/¼ oz	**wholemeal flour**	15 g/½ oz
½	**kiwi fruit, peeled and very thinly sliced**	1

ONE

1. Place the blackcurrants, honey, lemon juice and water in a bowl. Cover and microwave on HIGH for 2–3 minutes until soft. Purée in a blender then sieve to remove any seeds and skin.

2. Place the flour in a bowl and mix to a smooth paste with a little of the blackcurrant purée. Gradually add the remaining purée and microwave on HIGH for 1–2 minutes until thickened, stirring every ½ minute to keep the dessert smooth.

3. Spoon into a serving dish and float the kiwi slices on top. Serve with whipped cream.

TWO

1. Place the blackcurrants, honey, lemon juice and water in a bowl. Cover and microwave on HIGH for 3–4 minutes until soft. Purée in a blender then sieve to remove any seeds and skin.

2. Place the flour in a bowl and mix to a smooth paste with a little of the blackcurrant purée. Gradually add the remaining purée and microwave on HIGH for 1½–2 minutes until thickened, stirring every ½ minute to keep the dessert smooth.

3. Spoon into a serving dish and float the kiwi slices on top. Serve with whipped cream.

INDEX